God Doesn't Need a Badge

Rick Maruniak

ISBN 978-1-0980-4747-4 (paperback)
ISBN 978-1-0980-4748-1 (digital)

I have tried to recreate events, locales and conversations from my memories of them. In order to maintain their anonymity, in some instances, I have changed the names of individuals and places. Any resemblance to actual persons living or dead, or actual events is purely coincidental.

Christian Faith Publishing, Inc.
832 Park Avenue
Meadville, PA 16335
www.christianfaithpublishing.com

Printed in the United States of America

Contents

Introduction...5

Chapter 1: Pay Attention......................................7

Chapter 2: Anna..13

Chapter 3: Nick..27

Chapter 4: What Are the Odds? 44

Chapter 5: Praying to Get Robbed............................52

Chapter 6: Why Change? 62

Chapter 7: The Bike Story....................................68

Chapter 8: The Apology 86

Chapter 9: What I Wanted and What I Got 117

Chapter 10: Bongo Music.....................................135

Chapter 11: What I Learned about Prayer and
            Paying Attention 146

Chapter 12: God Was Paying Attention to Me 152

Chapter 13: Strategy for Paying Attention 161

Chapter 14: This Is Not about Me 173

Chapter 15: Look for a Miracle 175

Chapter 16: Prayer Unit 177

Chapter 17: The End and the Beginning..................179

Introduction

The tools that the police use in the twenty-first century to investigate crime are cutting-edge. As a retired police detective, I can tell you that I was able to use all the tools to investigate and solve hundreds of crimes. Some of these crimes were easy to solve because the criminals would leave a lot of evidence behind. Sometimes they would leave a fingerprint or DNA, or a video camera would capture the incident. Eyewitnesses would also help solve crimes.

The hardest crimes to investigate are the crimes with no evidence or witnesses and no investigative leads. There isn't a detective alive that has a 100 percent success rate in solving crime.

I want you to know that I met the greatest detective, and he directed me and taught me how to solve the unsolvable crimes. The funny thing is, I knew him the whole time, but did not realize that he would help me. All I had to do was ask.

The best thing about this detective is that he knows who committed every crime since the beginning of time. His name is Jesus.

As you read the stories in this book, you will discover that it is written to help you understand the power of prayer and strengthening your faith in God.

Chapter 1

Pay Attention

When I became a police officer, one of the first things I learned was to pay attention. Paying attention to what is going on while working can be a matter of life and death. I learned this skill by practice. I believe that police officers are some of the best at paying attention. Police officers can pay attention to several things at one time.

When I was a rookie officer, I was told to listen to the police radio. It was explained to me that I needed to know when police radio was calling, because this meant that they were giving us an assignment. The veteran training officer also explained to me that I should know the location of every other police officer on duty, and the location of their assignment. He said the reason to pay attention was in case an officer called for help; we could respond immediately without asking police radio where they were. It could be the difference between saving a life and losing one.

I was trained to always know where we were. I know this might sound funny to some, but knowing your location during the day and night is difficult when you are constantly on patrol. I was told that anything can happen at any time. One moment I could be on patrol, and the next second I could be flagged down and out of the car chasing a suspect who might have a gun. This is not the time to ask the person you're chasing what street they are on. I also had to be aware of direction. Was I traveling north, south, east, or west?

Paying attention also came in handy when I had to testify in court. An attorney would attempt to discredit a police officer if he couldn't remember certain things that happened during an arrest.

Paying attention was a new skill for me. I got good at it. It didn't come easy. I had to practice every day. I made up my mind to pay attention, and I changed. It made me a better police officer and detective, and was beneficial later in my career in SWAT.

I wish I had applied my new skill to my life once I became a born-again Christian in 1982. I didn't realize that God was performing miracles in my life. I have read about all the miracles that God had done in the Bible. I believe in every single one of them. I never thought that God would do a miracle for me. Once I started to pay attention, I started to see miracles.

I'm sure that all Christians have seen a miracle at one time in their life. The question to ask is, was I paying attention? You see, I didn't start paying attention until God answered my prayer and showed me a miracle twenty-four hours after I prayed. Once I realized that God had done a miracle involving me, I was overwhelmed and blown away. When I stop and think about God and realize that he had listened to my prayer request and answered it, I was amazed.

I have heard stories about people who have been diagnosed with cancer and miraculously healed. Have you ever heard a story about car accidents where a victim is helped by a stranger who is later believed to be an angel? You would think that these miracles would be on the front page of the newspaper and the top story on the news. The headlines should read, "GOD DOES ANOTHER MIRACLE." God is good. God is good all the time.

When I read the Bible, I wonder what the witnesses to God's miracles were thinking. Do you think that they were amazed? What do you think happened when Jesus raised Lazarus from the dead? What do you think the doctors said? Do you think the apostles started to pay attention after all the miracles they witnessed? Think about it. How would you have felt after you witnessed Jesus walk on water or control the weather? I think that I would start to pay close attention to Jesus, because you don't know what is going to happen next.

I believe a lot of Christians are missing out on what God has been doing for us in our life because they are not paying attention. You might not see Jesus walking on water or raising the dead, but I believe he has answered our prayers at one time or another and we have missed it.

The stories in this book are miracles from God. I am thankful that God woke me up to what he is doing in my life. I'm thankful that he made me pay attention.

When I first started to pray about solving criminal cases, I would not mention to my fellow detectives that I had asked God for help. God would then solve the case, and I would then tell them that I had prayed about this case. The responses I would get were mixed. I would get a lot of funny looks. You know what type of look I'm talking about. The looks that say *you're nuts or a religious fanatic*, or *you must be one of those born-again Christians*.

Some of the comments were funny too. The detective would say, "Oh, that's nice," or "You did a good job." The funny thing, though, is they never wanted to give the credit to God. I think some of them believed it was a coincidence or luck.

The looks and the comments didn't bother me. I knew exactly who was responsible for solving the crime. It was God. One of my favorite verses in the Bible is found in Romans 8:31: "If God is for me, who can be against me?"

I knew God was for me. That verse was my strength and is still my strength today.

The looks that I received from my fellow detectives did eventually change. Maybe some of the detectives thought that I was exaggerating about God answering my prayers. When a big case would come up and there seemed to be no good leads, I would purposely tell the other detectives that I was going to pray about the case. I figured that way, they would start to look to God and it would be a good time to witness to the detectives about trusting in Jesus.

God would then answer prayers, and when there was an arrest made, it was fun to show where God was involved. You see, I initially thought that I was the only one praying, but later realized that mothers were praying for their sons or daughters. I also learned that churches were praying. Victims of crime were praying for answers.

When you announce that you are praying for answers, people will watch for the results. They start paying attention. When I announced that I was praying to God about cases, I knew people were watching. Good detectives want to solve cases. Once the detectives were paying attention and realized that God was involved, their attitude changed. I remember a detective explaining to me about a case he had. He said that it was a case with no leads. He explained that a female had been raped and almost beaten to death and left in the back of a truck. He then asked me if I would pray about this case. I knew at that time that he was paying attention. He didn't ask me quietly or when we were alone. He asked me in front of the whole detective unit.

The funny thing is that he initially thought that I had a direct line to God. I believe a lot of people are like that. They are not sure how to have a relationship with God and they believe you have some special relationship because you go to church or you don't swear.

The reason I have a relationship with God is because I started paying attention to other Christians. I knew who they were before they were Christians and I saw changed lives after they had a relationship with Christ. I'm glad I paid attention. I wanted what they had.

My advice to anyone reading this book is to start paying attention. Start now. When you start to pay attention to your prayer life and looking for God in everything, your life will change dramatically. Practice paying attention. It changed me.

Chapter 2

Anna

In 1982, my life changed dramatically. That was the year I asked Jesus to forgive me and to come into my life and save me. Prior to 1982, my life was a mess. From the day I was saved, I felt like a new person. Jesus said, "I have come so you can have life and have life more abundant" (John 10:10). I did have life more abundant. From that day in 1982, I began to pray. I felt that God was listening to me and he would answer every prayer. The sad thing back then was that I wasn't paying attention. My life was changing daily, and God was teaching me that he had a plan for my life.

I can look back now and see that God has shown me that he was watching over me. I just wish I was paying attention. God placed people into my life at just the right time.

In 1986, I met my wife, Laura. I had been praying for a Christian girlfriend for a few years. I lived in the downstairs of a double house, and the upstairs was vacant. Laura answered the for-rent ad and ended up renting the house. I didn't know at that time that God had answered my prayer for a girlfriend. The funny thing, we didn't start to date until she moved out. I saw her after she moved out at a restaurant. I asked her out and we have been together since. God is good. He sent the perfect woman.

Laura and I got married in 1987. The day we got married, I started a job at the Cleveland Justice Center. I was working in the police radio room. Laura was attending college and we could barely make ends meet financially. I then took a second job driving a taxi. I would work on my off days.

What I didn't realize when I started to drive a taxi was how stressful and dangerous the job was. I would drive for twelve hours at a time, and if I was lucky, I would break even after I paid for the rental of the taxi. At that time, I didn't know the city of Cleveland like I know it now. I would get lost or go the wrong way. I met a lot of interesting people. Some people were kind, and others not so kind.

The dangerous part of driving a taxi is not knowing who is sitting behind you. There were times that I felt like I was going to get hit over the head or shot in the back. There were areas in the city that I felt were risky to go into.

Once you get a fare sitting in the back seat of the taxi, it's hard to tell the person that you don't feel comfortable going to that neighborhood. Against my better judgment, I went. God was watching out for me. He later showed me when I became a police officer how he took care of me when I was driving a taxi. Remember, I wasn't paying attention.

I started to get better driving a taxi, but at times I would get angry if I got a lousy tip or if I would pick someone up and it was a short ride. I realized that the longer the ride, the more money you would get. I would also get angry if a person paid with a voucher. A voucher would be good for a certain monetary amount. With a voucher you would normally not get a tip.

Even though I was working two jobs, Laura and I were having a hard time getting ahead. We would have conversations about buying a house once she finished school. Laura was going to school to become a teacher. I remember counting pennies or collecting pop cans for scrap just to get a few dollars.

When I started driving a taxi, I had no idea that God had a miracle waiting for me. Like I said, I wasn't paying attention. Sometimes we get caught up in life and are not looking for God to be involved. My partner Joe would say it's the opera syndrome, "me, me, me, me." I thought I was in control when I got the job driving the taxi, and that I was in control when I got the job working in police radio.

I wasn't in control of anything. I know that now. God had me right where he wanted me. God is in control.

Like I said, my wife and I wanted to buy a house with virtually no money. I am not sure of the exact date, but I remember praying with my wife before we went to bed. The prayer was a simple prayer. We asked God if he would help us find a house to buy that we could afford. This was the first time we had prayed that prayer. We both went to bed not knowing what was in store for us the following day.

The morning after we prayed for a house started like any other day. Even though we had asked God to help us, I really wasn't expecting a house to fall from the sky. I wasn't paying attention. I had no idea if God was going to answer our prayer this day or years from now. I decided that since I was off from work at police radio, I was going to try to make some extra money driving a taxi.

I went to the taxi company and picked up my vehicle. When I turned on the radio, I immediately heard the dispatcher giving out assignments. If you wanted the assignment and if you were the first person to press the microphone button, you would get the assignment. The dispatcher would give you the address and the name of the person you were to pick up. You were then responsible for picking up the person and taking them to their destination. I must admit, I was not very good at responding on the microphone. I wasn't fast, and I couldn't initially figure out the location where the person needed to be picked up. I would usually try to pick up fares on the west side of Cleveland. I was familiar with the street names since this was the area where I grew up.

I heard the dispatcher call out a run that was close to where I was located, and I immediately pushed the microphone button. To my surprise, I was the fastest, and the run was given to me. This was my first run of the day. The dispatcher told me to go to Metro Hospital and pick up a lady named Anna who would be at a certain location at the hospital.

While I was driving to the hospital, I started to daydream about how far of a ride I would be taking Anna. The farther the ride, the better for me, because it would be more money. It was the first fare of the day and it would have been nice to start the day with a long ride.

I pulled up to the hospital at the front door and went inside. I looked for Anna and could not find her. I started to get upset because I expected her to be waiting for me at the front door. I asked myself, who would call for a taxi and not be there when it showed up? I then checked at the front desk to see if anyone had called for a taxi. I was told no.

I was now angry and decided to leave the hospital. Driving a taxi is a hustle job. Wasting time cost money, and now I felt like my fare wasn't at the hospital and I had just wasted thirty minutes when I could have answered other taxi radio runs.

I got into my cab and started to drive away. I then heard the dispatcher over the radio call my car number. I responded and was told that Anna was waiting for me in a certain area of the hospital and I needed to go to that area to personally pick her up. I felt a little weird when the dispatcher called me, because I was driving away, and it felt like she knew that I was leaving. I remember thinking, *Oh well, I guess I'll have to go get her.*

I drove back to the front door of the hospital and went directly to where Anna was located. There were a lot of people in the area, so I called out for Anna. An older lady answered, and I introduced myself and asked if she had called for a taxi. Anna said yes. She told me she was going home, and she had a voucher to pay me. When Anna gave me the voucher, I immediately looked to see how much I was going to get paid. It was $12.00. I wasn't very happy. I felt like I had wasted my time answering the dispatcher for this fare.

I helped Anna into the taxi and started our ride to the address on the voucher. Anna looked small and frail. She seemed around eighty years old. I wondered why she was in the hospital, but I didn't ask her. I heard the dispatcher give several more runs to pick up fares in the area where I usually worked. I became more frustrated because I had Anna in my back seat, and I couldn't answer any of the calls. I was missing out on making money.

I was driving with Anna for about fifteen minutes when I heard her say, "Driver?"

I said, "Yes?"

Anna said she had forgotten her glasses at the hospital, and she needed them. Anna didn't know then, but I was starting to overheat. I thought, *Are you kidding me right now?*

I turned the cab around and headed back to the hospital. On the ride back to the hospital, I didn't say a word to Anna. I didn't know if she could feel the cold shoulder I was giving her. What I thought was going to be the start of a good taxi day was turning out to be a bad day.

When I arrived at the hospital, I told Anna to wait in the taxi and I would run inside and get her glasses. Anna said okay and told me where she had left them. I went into the hospital and found them. I returned to the taxi and gave them to her.

She was very happy and said thank you. I asked Anna if she had left anything else at the hospital, and she said no.

I drove away thinking that I didn't want to pick up another patient from the hospital for a long time. I continued my silent treatment with Anna while I was driving her to her destination. I didn't feel like talking. I just wanted to do my job and get her to her destination as quickly as possible. I wanted to drop her off so I could get another fare.

I was about halfway to Anna's destination when I again heard Anna say, "Driver?" I didn't want to answer her this time. I knew if she said she had left something else at the hospital, I was going to be rude. I didn't want to be rude, especially to an older female, but I didn't want to go back to the hospital.

I slowly said, "Yes, ma'am?"

Anna asked me if I knew why she was in the hospital. I told her that I didn't know. Anna said she was at home cooking in her kitchen when she slipped and fell. She had been on her floor for three days before anyone found her. She had broken her hip.

I immediately started to feel guilty about the way I was treating her. It never dawned on me why Anna was at the hospital. I told her I was sorry to hear that she had fallen and broken her hip. At this time, my mood changed, and we had a good conversation.

I asked Anna if she had family or neighbors who could check up on her. Anna said she has a son who lived in Texas. Her son wanted her to move to Texas and live with him, and she wanted to move in with her son. What Anna told me next really amazed me and blew me away. Anna said she was going to sell her house and asked me if I knew anyone who might be interested in buying.

I immediately said I might be interested. Of course I was interested. I remembered that my wife and I had asked God the night before for a house we could afford. I explained to Anna that my wife and I were looking for a house and we had prayed the night before. It's funny, one minute I was in a hurry to get Anna home so I could drop her off and pick up my next fare, and the next minute I wanted to get Anna home so I could look at her house. I was starting to pay attention.

Anna and I talked about her house for the rest of the ride. I was getting anxious about what her house might look like. I wondered if it was a house I could afford. The antic- ipation was killing me. I wondered if God had answered our prayer.

I pulled the taxi into Anna's driveway and saw a small white bungalow house. From the outside, it appeared to be well maintained. I noticed that she had a one-car garage and a small backyard. I remember thinking that I could see myself living here.

Anna told me to come into the house with her. She wanted to show me the inside of the home. I walked into the front door and found myself in the living room. On the wall were pictures of John F. Kennedy and Martin Luther King, Jr. The house was decorated modestly and in need of a fresh coat of paint.

When I looked to my right, I saw Anna's kitchen. I immediately felt ashamed and sad. I pictured Anna lying on the floor for three days, alone and helpless. I felt ashamed at the way I had treated her. I didn't treat her with the respect that she deserved. I didn't take the time to consider who she was and where she had come from and why she was in the hospital. I wasn't paying attention. I believe God was teaching me a lesson.

Anna showed me the rest of the home from top to bottom. I told Anna that I liked the house and I was interested in buying it, but my wife would want to look at the house. I decided to bring my wife back the next day. I said goodbye to Anna and got back into my taxi.

I didn't answer the radio to pick up any fares when I left Anna's home. I drove around in the taxi, pondering what had just happened. I was excited because I felt that Anna's home was right for my wife and me. I remember thinking that I couldn't be blessed by God if I wanted to. God was trying to bless me by meeting Anna, and all I could think about was a little bit of money that I was losing in fares. God sent me to the hospital, and I tried to leave because I couldn't find Anna right away. I remembered that I was leaving the hospital and I heard the dispatcher tell me to basically go back into the hospital. I wondered, was it the dispatcher calling me, or was it God?

I thought about the odds of praying for a home that we could afford and then the next day picking up Anna. I felt that this was an answer to prayer. I felt a little frightened. My wife and I didn't have much money. I didn't ask Anna how much she wanted for her home. I know this sounds stupid now, but I thought maybe God sent me to a house that I couldn't afford to buy. I needed help to sort this out, so I decided to drive back to my house and tell my wife what had just happened.

When I arrived at my house, I went inside trying to act calm. The first thing I asked my wife was if she remembered praying for a house. She said yes, last night. I told her that I might have a house to buy. I then explained to her how I met Anna at the hospital and that she wanted to sell her house. I told her that we could look at the house the next day. Laura was excited and asked me a lot of questions about Anna and her house. I didn't have a lot of answers for Laura. We talked for another hour, and then I went back to work.

The next night at work, I felt different. My thought process changed. I started to relax. The people I picked up in my taxi seemed different to me. I realized that everyone we meet has a story and deserves to be treated with respect. I realized that God was teaching me a lesson. The Bible says in Hebrews 13:2, "Do not neglect to show hospitality to strangers, for by so doing some people have shown hospitality to angels without knowing it." I knew that when I first met Anna, I wasn't very hospitable. I wondered if Anna was an angel.

I finished the night driving the taxi and went home. My wife was up, and we talked about Anna. Laura wanted me to go over every detail again. I could see she was excited. I told her that if she liked the house and if we could afford it, we should buy it. Laura said that Anna was probably an angel. I laughed and I wondered if there were any visible signs to recognizing angels here on earth. I was going to look for signs tomorrow when we went to look at the house.

I remember going to bed that night and feeling restless. I fell asleep thinking about God and how fast everything was moving. I wasn't sure if I was ready to move this fast. I had a lot of questions. I knew if God was involved, everything was going to be okay.

The following day, Laura and I went to look at the house. I didn't have any idea if my wife would like the house. It's weird, I felt that God had answered our prayer, but I didn't know what would happen if Laura didn't like it. Well, Laura did like the house. When we went inside, Anna gave us a tour of her home, and after that, we sat and talked to Anna.

Anna was a good salesman. She explained how she wanted to sell the house. Anna told us that she wanted to sell the house on a five-year land contract. Anna wanted five thousand dollars down and we were to make monthly payments. At the end of the five years, she wanted the balance. I explained that we only had two thousand dollars in our savings and we couldn't give her the five thousand dollars. Anna said that she would take the two thousand dollars now and then after one year we would have to give her the remaining three thousand dollars down payment. Anna asked if we knew what the current interest rates on home loans were. I told her that I believed the rates were around 10 percent. Anna told us we could have an 8 percent interest rate for the five years.

I looked at Laura, and I could see she was amazed. I asked what she thought, and she said we should buy the house. We then told Anna we wanted to buy the house. We did tell Anna that we had prayed the night before and asked God for a house. Anna said she believed that God answers prayers. Anna was truly an angel.

God orchestrated this deal. He worked out every detail for us. I believe this 100 percent. This was truly a miracle. It still amazes me to this day. God, the creator of heaven and earth, heard our prayer and said yes. I love the way he answered the prayer and, at the same time, taught me several lessons.

Anna sold us her home. I'm not sure if she really knew she was involved in this miracle at the time. Anna passed away a few years later, and I believe she now knows that she was used by God.

God used Anna to help my wife and me, and I will never forget how this changed our life. I want to stress this point. When we are living our lives, we need to pay attention. God is involved in everything we do. When you stop and look for God, he will reveal himself. We need to ask this question: How can I live my life day after day and look for God?

Well, I believe that Anna wanted to help someone, even though she was the one who needed help. She had a servant attitude. God used her because she wanted to be used. Anna was an angel. Maybe Anna was paying attention.

Chapter 3

Nick

In 1989, we moved into Anna's home, and that was the year I became a police officer. I did pray and ask God if he would let me become a police officer. I now know that this was God's plan for my career. I believe God wanted me to be a police officer, and I would like to say that I was paying attention early on and looking for God, but much of the time, I wasn't paying attention. I know I must have missed several opportunities during this time. I realize now that when God puts you in a position, it's so he can use you. We should see the bigger picture. We should be ready to let God lead us and we must pay attention to every situation and what God is telling us to do.

I had spent the past nine years working in uniform and working with a partner in a zone car. The police district I was working in had an opening for a detective. I put in for the job and I got it. It was a suit-and-tie job and I could work the day shift from Monday through Friday. It was a perfect fit for a family. My wife would take our kids to school in the morning and I would pick them up after work. We would all be off on the weekends. I believe God was watching out for me with my work schedule. There are not a lot of police-related jobs with that type of schedule. The best part of the schedule was that I could attend church on Sunday.

When I started my job in the detective bureau, I soon realized that there was a lot to learn. I observed the veteran detectives and how they put their cases together. I also learned that it was important to investigate every lead and to speak to everyone that might be involved, even if you think it is not important. The last thing that a detective wants is to have a defense attorney ask during trial if you followed up on a lead and you must tell the attorney no. The veteran detectives knew what to expect and did a great job teaching me about a crime scene and what to do with evidence collected.

I later realized that a detective's work never ends. You could investigate a crime and identify a suspect and make an arrest and then you must appear in front of a grand jury. The grand jury hears the facts of your investigation and then votes true bill or no bill. If the grand jury votes true bill, the case will be forwarded for trial. Most of the cases forwarded for trial do get settled with plea bargains and do not go to trial. The prosecutor handling the criminal cases usually subpoenas the investigating detective prior to any plea bargain and always before a trial begins. I have seen detectives working their cases and appearing in the grand jury and then consulting with prosecutors and appearing in court for trial all in the same day. Busy, busy, busy.

The detectives I worked with were hardworking. Each detective would handle between 150 to 200 cases a year. We would share information and assist each other. I learned different techniques on how to interview victims and interrogate suspects. I learned how to read body language and how to tell when someone was not telling the truth during an interview.

The most fun I had while working in the detective bureau was during the interview. There is great satisfaction when a suspect in a crime confesses during an interview. The main reason that you want a suspect to confess to committing the crime is so you can have 100 percent satisfaction that an innocent person is not going to jail.

God taught me many lessons when I interviewed suspects. Many times, when I interviewed suspects, God was telling me, *This could have been you getting interviewed.* I knew what God had saved me from and what he meant. I knew what to say to the person I was interviewing. Many times, I knew that these people were going to jail for a long time. Sometimes I would pray with them.

God later taught me that he answers prayers for the people I had arrested. God taught me that there are three verdicts. There is a guilty verdict and a not-guilty verdict. There is also a guilty verdict, but God lets them off. Do you remember when you were younger, and you did something bad, and you prayed to God and made a promise that you would never do that again if God got you out of trouble? Well, it still happens today. I have been involved in cases where the evidence was overwhelming, and the suspect was found not guilty. I later learned that the suspect's mother was in court and praying during the trial. Did God answer her prayer? I believe, yes. God is involved in everything.

Once I started to pay attention and look for God at work, I saw God everywhere. I realized that I should ask God to assist me with my investigations. This story I'm about to tell you is true. The funny thing about this story is, it takes place at a doughnut shop. The owner of the doughnut shop is named Nick.

I had been a detective for a few years when I first met Nick. Like I said, Nick owned a doughnut shop in a rough area in Cleveland. Nick had been robbed two times in one year. The robberies took place during the day when Nick was open for business. Two males came into his doughnut shop and showed a gun and demanded money. The males wore face masks and gloves. A detective from my unit was assigned these two cases and investigated the robberies.

The detective worked the case for a year and did not come up with any leads or arrests. The detective handling this investigation had officially closed his investigation. At the time, I did not have any knowledge about the robberies.

I arrived at the detective bureau like any other morning and saw that I had received an assignment to investigate. I was told by my supervisor that a doughnut shop was robbed, and this was the third time it had been robbed at gunpoint in a year. My supervisor explained about the prior two robberies and told me that another detective from our unit did investigate the first two robberies. My supervisor told me that he wanted me to investigate this robbery because the initial detective was on vacation. I was also told that the owner, Nick, was upset with the police because an arrest had not been made.

I could understand that Nick was upset. He had been held up at gunpoint three times in one year. I immediately contacted Nick by phone and asked if he could come to the detective bureau so he could give a statement about what took place at the doughnut shop. Nick stated that he could not come to the detective bureau because he was the only person working. I told Nick that I would come to the doughnut shop the following day and I could take his statement there. Nick agreed, and we set up a time. I hung up the phone and told my supervisor about the arrangements I made with Nick.

I went back to work. I was finishing up my shift getting ready to go home when I received a call from Nick. He was yelling into the phone. Nick said he had just gotten robbed again, and this time they took a shot at him. Nick said he wanted me to come to the doughnut shop right then. I asked Nick if he called 911 to report the crime and he said yes. I tried to explain that I was getting off work and I was responsible for picking up my kids from school and didn't have anyone I could call for this emergency. Nick continued to yell at me, blaming me for not doing anything about the past three robberies. Nick was yelling at me like he was my father. I understood Nick's anger, and I tried to explain that I had just received the case eight hours prior. Nick called me lazy and a lousy detective. I told him I was sorry and told him to make the report when the police arrived, and I would come to the doughnut shop tomorrow. Nick hung up on me.

I immediately informed my supervisor about this fresh robbery. I remembered that I was scheduled to work the second shift the next day. I asked my supervisor if I could come to work earlier so I could go and do my interview with Nick. I explained that I had made an appointment with Nick and forgot that I was working the second shift. My supervisor gave me the okay.

I left work to pick my kids up, and when we arrived back home, I checked with my supervisor about the robbery and to make sure that the police took a report and that the crime scene was processed for fingerprints and photographs. I was told that it was. I couldn't stop thinking about Nick and how he was yelling at me out of frustration on the phone.

It was now that I decided to do something different. I thought about God and how he answered my prayer for a house. I decided that I would pray and ask God for help solving the robberies with Nick. My prayer was simple. It went something like this: "Dear Lord, please help me to solve this crime and show me who is robbing Nick. He has been robbed three times in the last year and this time they shot at him." I laughed to myself when I told God what happened. I knew he knew exactly what happened. I also explained that Nick was yelling at me. He knew that too. This was the first time I asked God for help solving a crime. I can laugh now. I was asking God to help me solve a crime. It was a doughnut shop.

I went to bed thinking about Nick and I woke up thinking about Nick. When I said that a detective's work is never done, the main reason is you never stop thinking about your cases. I thought about cases when I was off on my weekends, away at vacation, and every holiday.

I went to work and picked up a vehicle and a portable police radio. I told my supervisor that I was going to the doughnut shop to interview Nick. While I was driving, I wondered what Nick looked like and how he would treat me. The last thing Nick did was hang up the phone on me. I wondered if he was still mad.

When I arrived at the doughnut shop, I realized that I had not been in this shop at all when I worked in a zone car. The shop was on a main street with a front entrance. I parked my car in front and went inside the shop. I introduced myself to a counter clerk and asked to see Nick. I was told that Nick had an appointment and was not there. I got a little frustrated and asked the clerk if he could contact Nick. He said no, he didn't know how to contact him.

I asked the clerk if he knew what happened the day of the robbery. He told me he was working during the robbery. He said he was in the back of the shop when two men came into the doughnut shop wearing a mask to cover half their face. He said one of the men pointed a gun at him and demanded money. The man with the gun fired a round into the wall above the clerk's head. He said he gave them a cigar box of money that was in the back, and after they took the money, they left out of the back door of the shop. I asked him if would recognize these two men if he saw them again. He said no, because they were wearing masks. He then gave me a physical description of the two men.

I asked the clerk if I could go to the back room, and he said okay. We went to the back and I wanted him to go over everything that happened again. I wanted to see where they kept the money and where the bullet hole was. I wanted to know if they touched anything in the back to look for fingerprints. He told me they were wearing gloves. He showed me the back door they ran out of. He also described the gun that was used.

I got all the information I needed from the clerk and asked him to step outside with me. We went out the back door of the shop, and I noticed a light covering of snow with footprints coming to and from the shop's back door. I asked the worker if he knew which way the two men ran, and he said he didn't know. I asked the worker a couple more questions, and then he said that he had to go back into the shop because he now had some customers.

The worker went inside the shop, and I stayed outside. I was looking at the footprints. They stopped at a fence about thirty feet from the store. If you jumped the fence, it led to the backyard of a house and into a residential neighborhood. My plan was to go to the house and check for more footprints.

I was standing in the back of the doughnut shop. I was wearing a suit and tie and had my police radio in my back pocket. I had nothing visible on me that would identify me as a detective. The reason I'm telling you what I'm wearing is because as I was standing out back, a man came out from behind the fence. He startled me. He was fifteen feet away from me. He looked right at me, lifted his jacket at his waist, and took out an automatic handgun. He dropped it on the ground and took off running.

That freaked me out. He could have shot me. This was the first and only time that someone got the drop on me. I was thankful he started to run. I don't believe he knew I was a detective because of the way I was dressed. I remember the look on his face. He looked like he committed a crime and was trying to get away or the police were chasing him.

I picked up the gun and started to follow him. I got on my police radio and told them that I was chasing a man and that he had just thrown a gun down in the back of the doughnut shop. A police officer heard my radio broadcast and responded over radio that he was sent to a boarded-up house because of a suspicious male, and when he pulled up, the man took off running and jumped a fence by the doughnut shop.

I continued to follow this man, and I watched as he took off his jacket while running and threw it down. I saw that underneath his jacket he had a bulletproof vest on. He then took off his bulletproof vest and threw that on the ground. I followed the man into a restaurant, and when I entered, I didn't see him. I asked a worker if he saw anyone run inside, and he pointed to the lady's bathroom. I opened the door to the lady's bathroom and had a short struggle with the man. I was able to handcuff him.

I was walking back with this man the same route that he took. I wanted to recover the vest and his jacket. I picked up the bulletproof vest and his jacket. Inside the jacket pockets were blue latex gloves, bullets, and a half mask. I now believed that this man was responsible for robbing the doughnut shop.

When I got back to the doughnut shop, a marked zone car was waiting for me. I asked if I could put this man in the back of his zone car. I explained to the officer that I believed this man was responsible for robbing the doughnut shop the day before.

I went inside the doughnut shop and spoke with the clerk, whom I had just interviewed. I explained to him what happened when he went back inside the shop. I told him I have someone arrested and he is in the back of the zone car. I knew he couldn't identify him because of the mask. I asked him to come to the zone car and look at the man in the back and just nod his head yes. I wanted the arrested man to think that he was identified.

The clerk came out, and when we opened the door so he could view the man, he immediately nodded his head yes. The clerk went back inside the shop, and I spoke to the officer outside of the zone car so the arrested man could hear us talking. I told the officer that the clerk had positively identified this man as the one who had robbed him and shot at him yesterday. I asked the officer if he could take this man back to the detective bureau so I could interview him.

On my way, back to the detective bureau, I prayed. I asked God for this man to give me a written confession. I really didn't have him arrested for the robbery. He was arrested for having the gun. I thought about how I wanted to interview this man and wondered if he believed that he was identified as the person who robbed the doughnut shop. It was a bluff, and I hoped that he fell for it.

When I arrived back at the detective bureau, I grabbed all the reports that were connected to the doughnut shop and reviewed them. I wanted to know if this man might have been involved in the prior robberies. The suspect descriptions in the reports were all very similar. I wondered, could this man be responsible for all the robberies?

I thought about how I should interview this man. The interview is a tricky thing. You try to figure out what the person you're interviewing is about. You want the person to trust you as much as possible. It's important to know as much as you can about the person's background. Where they live and who they live with. Where they attended school and what they believe in will help during the interview. The more you know about them the better.

It's also important to watch how they respond to basic questions. The reason to watch is so you can get a feeling how they react to questions when they tell the truth.

Basic questions asked are, "What is your name? Date of birth? Where do you live or work?" This way you can compare how they react when confronted with questions about crimes they committed.

I started the interview by introducing myself. I found out that his name was James. I explained to James that I was investigating the robberies at the doughnut shop. To my surprise, James did admit to the crime. James told me that he was going to rob the doughnut shop again that day, but he saw the police pull up when he was at the fence, and he took off running. That is when I saw him, followed him, and then arrested him in the bathroom.

James also admitted to robbing the doughnut shop two times prior. I knew that there were two people who had been involved. James also gave me the name of the second person involved. James gave me information about the robberies that only the person who committed the crime would know. I felt confident that James was responsible.

I stated to think about all the work ahead of me. I knew I needed to do a search warrant at James's home to recover stolen property. I knew I had to get an arrest warrant for James's accomplice. I also had to bring Nick and any witnesses to the detective bureau and take their statements. I also had to consult a prosecutor and put together all the reports. What I didn't know was that my supervisor, Sergeant Bruce, was reviewing crime reports with similar suspect descriptions, when the suspects wore a half mask and blue rubber gloves and used a handgun.

I heard a knock on the door of the interview room, and Sergeant Bruce walked in and asked to speak with me for a second. I stepped outside and noticed that Sergeant Bruce had several more criminal case files in his hand. Sergeant Bruce told me to ask James about several other crimes in the same neighborhood. Sergeant Bruce believed that James was involved in these crimes. A lot of police officers believe that when someone gets arrested for a crime, it isn't the first crime that they have committed, but it's the first time they have gotten caught.

I knew James had already confessed to three robberies, so I reviewed the crime files that Sergeant Bruce gave me and asked James if he was involved. James did admit to being involved, and now I learned that there were several other suspects with James during these crimes. James gave me several names of people that he committed crimes with.

James admitted to robbing and shooting a pizza delivery driver. James and his friends ordered a pizza and had it delivered to an abandoned house, and when the driver arrived, they shot him in the leg and took his money. James and his friends also went to several fast food restaurants and jumped the counters armed with weapons and robbed the restaurants.

When I finished my interview with James, I realized again how much work I had to do. There were a lot more people to arrest and a lot more people to interview. James went to jail, and I was ready to go home after a long day.

While I was driving on the way home, I started to think about what happened. First, I knew I prayed about the doughnut shop robberies the day before asking God for help. Then I went to the doughnut shop, and Nick was gone. I went to the back of the shop, and that's when James ran out in front of me. Then, after arresting James, he gave me a full confession and admitted to several other crimes. What are the odds? The odds are tremendous. I knew then that God had answered my prayer.

I arrived at home and told my wife everything that happened. I told her God answered my prayer request. I also told my wife that the only bad thing about my prayer request was that God not only solved the doughnut shop robberies, but he also solved several other crimes. I told her when God is involved, there is going to be a lot of work.

When I had time alone with God, I thanked him for answering my prayer request. I felt overwhelmed because I knew without a doubt that God was with me. It's a powerful feeling when the creator shows you a miracle, and in that miracle, God includes you. Wow. I would never be the same, and I knew it.

I went to work the next morning knowing I had a lot of work to do. Before I did any work, I sat with several other coworkers and Sergeant Bruce. Police officers like to tell stories of their experiences, especially if they are different from the norm. My coworkers asked what had happened yesterday. They already knew that James had a gun and a bulletproof vest, and he had confessed to several crimes. I told them that when I got the case and Nick got robbed again, I prayed and asked God to help me. I even told them the prayer. I then explained everything and again asked, "What are the odds?"

I remember some of their faces after I told them God had answered my prayer request. As a detective, I was pretty good at reading body language. My friends were trying not to disrespect me by smirking or laughing. A couple of the other detectives just said, "Oh, that's good." I didn't care. I knew the truth and I was claiming it. In Romans 8:31, it says, "If God is for you, who can be against you?" I knew God was for me, and it didn't matter what anyone else thought about me.

I later had to testify in front of the grand jury about this incident. It was funny. I was sworn in to tell the truth. The prosecutor leads the grand jury and reviews the case file prior to the detective testifying. The prosecutor usually has an idea about what the official charges are. The prosecutor complimented me on doing a good job solving these crimes. He then asked me how I solved these crimes.

I told him and the grand jury that the first thing I did was pray about this case. The look on the prosecutor's face was hilarious. I was watching the jurors' faces also. Some were nodding in agreement and others were looking at me funny. After I made that statement, I sensed the prosecutor was trying to rush me out of the room. I'm almost positive that praying to God and asking to solve a crime is not a probable cause for a grand jury.

Every crime that I presented to the grand jury that day, all suspects were indicted and later convicted and sent to jail.

What a whirlwind God had me on. I wondered if I should pray about other cases. Heck yeah, I should. The sky was the limit. I would never again investigate a crime the same old way. God was now my partner.

Chapter 4

What Are the Odds?

I finished with the doughnut shop investigation and felt like I had changed. I knew God had answered my prayer. I wanted to do things differently at work. God gave me a new outlook on work. I had always loved my job, but now God made it more exciting than ever. I went to work every day expecting a miracle. I also knew that God wanted me to tell people about what he did for me. I decided that if I had a case for which I prayed and asked God for help, I would tell my coworkers prior so they could see the miracle too. I was now paying attention.

I decided to ask God for help on a cold case where I had exhausted all my leads. The case was about six months old. I remember pulling the file from my desk and reading it. This case was a smash-and-grab robbery at a jewelry store. Glass cases were broken, and watches were taken. A witness to this crime could give a description of the suspect and a description of a vehicle used. The witness described the car as a gold Ford Crown Victoria with a temporary tag license in the rear window. The witness was able to write down the numbers of the temporary tag. I remember running the license plate on the computer and going to an apartment complex and finding the apartment empty. I spoke with the manager of the apartments and I was told that the person had moved without notice and had not left a forwarding address. I attempted to locate the owner of the vehicle and I never could find him. I had the name of the owner of the vehicle and the car used in this crime. It was not enough to get an arrest warrant for the owner, but he was a person of interest.

I held the case file in my hand, and while I was sitting at my desk at work, I said another prayer. I asked God for help solving this crime. I told him this was a cold case and I had exhausted all my leads. Once again, I laughed because I was telling God what he already knew. When I was done praying, I left the file on my desk. This time, I told my partner, Dale, that I had asked God for help on this cold case. I then left the office and went home.

The following day at work, I was sitting at my desk doing paperwork. A couple of hours had gone by when the sergeant who oversaw the strike force came into the office. He told me that his detectives had raided a dry cleaner's for drug sales, and they arrested several people.

He explained that he wanted to separate the people so they were not able to talk to each other. He then asked if he could put one of the arrested men handcuffed to my desk while the detectives did their interviews. I said it was okay. It was common to handcuff prisoners to a chair while a detective conducted an interview.

The strike force sergeant brought this man over to my desk and handcuffed him to my chair. The sergeant told him he would come back and get him when he was completed with the other interviews. I continued doing my paperwork with this man a few feet away from me. I did not speak to this man, and he didn't speak to me. He sat there for a few hours, and then the strike force sergeant came and got him so he could do his interview with him.

It was now getting close to the end of my shift and I was leaving the police station out the side door. I noticed that the strike force was still doing their investigation. As I was leaving, I noticed a few cars parked on the sidewalk. That was not unusual. Undercover detectives would park their cars on the sidewalk at times. What was unusual this time was that a gold Ford Crown Victoria was parked on the sidewalk.

I walked past the car and I heard the Holy Spirit tell me to look at the car. I looked at the car and I noticed that the car had a license plate on the trunk area, and in the rear window there was an outline of tape the size of a temporary tag. It looked like the temporary tag was removed and the tape outline was left. I remember thinking, *No way.* I was tired and I wanted to go home. I started to walk toward my car, and I heard the Holy Spirit say, "Look at the car, dummy." The Holy Spirit called me dummy. I then turned around and looked more closely at the car. I wrote down the license tag number and the vehicle identification number and went back into the detective bureau. I then looked at the cold case file that was on my desk. What I found out blew me away. The vehicle that I had been looking for the past six months was now parked on the sidewalk at the police station. Let me repeat that again. The vehicle I was looking for the past six months was parked on the sidewalk at the police station.

I couldn't believe what was happening. I had prayed twenty-four hours earlier asking God for help, and now the car was personally delivered to me. Now that's cool. I have looked for hundreds of vehicles in my career that were involved in crimes. I have never had one delivered to me at the police station. Who would believe what had just happened?

I then looked inside the police station to find out where the owner of the car was. I was surprised to find out that the owner of the car was one of the males that the strike force had arrested earlier. I went into the strike force office and located the owner of the car. Can you guess who the owner was? It was the man who was handcuffed to a chair by my desk. He was the man I had been looking for the past six months.

Now, think about that. What are the odds that I would pray about a six-month-old cold case, and twenty-four hours later, the person I'm looking for is in handcuffs sitting by my desk? Was this a coincidence? Was it fate, or bad luck, or good luck? Was it being at the right place at the right time? The only person who knew that I had prayed asking God for help was my partner Dale. The strike force had no idea I was looking for the vehicle and the owner. I don't think there is a person alive who could correctly give the odds of these things happening.

I knew one thing. God answered my prayer. I was overwhelmed. How do you deal with something like this emotionally? I felt like I was in shock. Sometimes it's hard to accept that God, the Creator of the Universe, is now helping me with my cases. Why me? I didn't know the answer. I wondered if it was for me, or for the person who got caught, or maybe the victim, or the other people around me whom I told about this miracle. It was something for me to think about once I calmed down and went home.

I had an interview with this man. I told him I had been looking for him because of the jewelry store robbery. I asked him if he thought it was unusual that he was handcuffed at my desk for a different crime. I told him that I had prayed and asked God for help. He looked at me like I was nuts. He then told me he had nothing to do with a robbery of a jewelry store. He then told me he wasn't going to answer any questions and wanted a lawyer. The interview ended. I would've liked to have gotten a confession, but that was okay. I now had his car and he was arrested by our strike force. He wasn't going anywhere soon. He was going to jail. I finished my paperwork and left the station to go home.

On my way home, I didn't turn on the car radio. I didn't want to be disturbed while I thought about what had just happened. I replayed the events in my head. I could feel God's presence in the car. I had a feeling of excitement in me. It wasn't about arresting this man for robbery. It was God. I felt God was with me. I used to wonder how the apostles felt when they witnessed a miracle. It had to be amazing. Imagine seeing people who were blind or crippled or sick with leprosy being healed by Jesus. I wondered what they thought when they were alone after witnessing these miracles. I went over my prayer in my head and realized that God had answered my prayer. Now, that is something to meditate about.

When I got home, I went into my bedroom and prayed. I didn't usually pray when I first arrived home from work. I felt I needed to thank God immediately. This time, I lay face-down on the floor. It was the first time I prayed like this. I remember reading about the commander of the Lord's army telling Joshua to take off his sandals, for the place he was standing on was holy. I felt God's presence, and I wanted to show respect. I don't know if you have ever felt like that before, but it's overwhelming. I wish I could feel this way every day. When I realized who was answering my prayer and how quickly, it overwhelmed me. I knew without a doubt that it was God. I went to bed that night thinking about God and what God had done.

The next day when I went to work, I told my boss Sergeant Bruce and my partner Dale what had happened. They both were a little shocked, to say the least. I explained that I had prayed, and that God had answered my prayer in less than twenty-four hours. I realized that I wanted to tell everyone what God had done.

I believe that the other detectives were starting to get curious and ask questions. I realized that God was using me, and I believe he wanted others to know what he was doing in my life. Every chance I got, I told my coworkers how God answered my prayers and solved these crimes. It also gave me an opening to talk about how I became a Christian. That was the biggest miracle of my life. God came into my life and changed me. God had a plan for my life.

In the Bible in Jeremiah 29:11, it says, "For I know the plans I have for you," declares the Lord, "plans to prosper you and not to harm you, plans to give you hope and a future." What are the odds that the Creator of the Universe, who is the God of gods, would have a plan for me, a police officer? I realize that what God was doing in my life was not to be kept a secret. I have told this story thousands of times, and I never get tired of telling about this miracle.

I completed all the paperwork connected to the jewelry store. I started thinking about other crimes that I could pray about. I wondered, would God answer every single prayer request about solving my criminal cases? My faith was growing stronger and stronger. I believed God would answer every single request. I was going to pay attention to my prayer life. I was going to ask God for help and immediately look for answers.

It's exciting when you realize that God wants to be involved in every part of your day. I loved my job, and God made my job even more exciting. When you wake up in the morning and you prepare for work, we should be asking God what it is he wants to accomplish with us today. What do you think the apostles thought when they woke up? They probably thought, *What are we going to do with Jesus today?* I'm sure that a day didn't go by that the apostles didn't witness a miracle, or a life changed when they were with Jesus. We can have that same opportunity. We need to pay attention.

Chapter 5

Praying to Get Robbed

I started praying about everything while I was in the detective bureau. I was praying about my criminal cases and the other detective's cases. God was answering my prayers. My faith was getting stronger every day. I would go to work expecting a miracle every day.

I remember I was looking for a man for whom I had an arrest warrant. I couldn't find him for a few months. I left work, and while driving home, I asked God to help me find this man. I arrived at work the next day, and the first thing I noticed at my desk was a red flashing light on my phone which indicated I had a voice message. I listened to the voice message. It was from a female who was the girlfriend of the man I was looking for. She said she knew I was looking for her boyfriend. She said they had gotten into an argument the night before and he assaulted her, and she now wanted to turn him in because she wanted him out of her house. Pretty amazing. I then went to her address and arrested her boyfriend. For the rest of my career, I would get excited seeing the flashing red light on my phone.

I was paying attention to everything around me and looking for God. I was praying about everything. I was praying for my family and coworkers. I would pray for victims of crime where I worked and in other cities. I would pray and then I would wait and watch to see how God would answer. How neat is that? Every day was exciting.

One of the most unusual prayer requests for me was to ask God to have a group of men approach me and rob me. I know, you're probably thinking that I'm nuts. Who would pray to get robbed?

I was working second shift at the detective bureau. Sergeant Terry from the vice unit came into the office and told me that he was setting up a detail to catch a group of men who were beating up people and robbing them as they were walking down the street. Sergeant Terry said that he had several cases in the same area and he believed they were the same group of males. Sergeant Terry said that he had used a police officer as a decoy a week prior with no luck. Sergeant Terry said that the police decoy he used was an instructor from the police gymnasium who was also a black belt in martial arts. Sergeant Terry believed that maybe the instructor looked too confident and that was the reason he didn't get approached.

Sergeant Terry told me he was going to use the instructor again today, but the instructor had to cancel for an emergency. Sergeant Terry asked me if I would be interested in being the decoy. Without thinking, I said yes. He thanked me and told me we would meet in his office in a couple of hours. He wanted to put me out when it got dark. He told me to change into different clothes. I told him okay and that I would see him in a couple of hours.

I started thinking about what I just volunteered for. I have never worked undercover, and I really didn't know how I should act as a decoy. I started thinking about different scenarios and what would I do if I was approached or robbed. I wondered what I would do if they had a gun or a knife. I wondered if anyone would recognize me since I had worked in that area for four years. These are the things I should have thought about before I volunteered. Oh well, it was too late now. I thought I will just make the best of this new experience.

I knew a lot of detectives who worked undercover and I knew it was dangerous work. As a police officer, I always wanted the people I dealt with to know I was a police officer. I didn't want any mistakes. The undercover detectives went to great lengths to hide their identity. They would grow their hair long and wear a beard and drive undercover cars to help them fit in. Some detectives would have fake identification and addresses. After doing all of that, they would then try to blend in with the criminals. I felt that they were probably some of the bravest police officers on the force. I couldn't imagine doing that type of work every day.

I went to my locker to change my clothes. Working in the detective bureau, we were required to wear a suit and tie. I changed into a pair of jeans and a hooded sweatshirt. I then went and got something to eat. When I finished eating, I felt I should pray. I asked God for protection. I told God that this assignment was new to me and I didn't know what to expect. I asked God that, if the people who were responsible for the robberies were out tonight, that they would approach me and rob me. What a request. I wanted these people to get caught.

I went to the vice unit, and we had a briefing with Sergeant Terry. There were about eight undercover vice detectives and four uniformed police officers in the office. Sergeant Terry explained what the mission was for the night and how we were going to monitor my activity. Sergeant Terry stated that I was going to wear a wire and that way they could monitor my conversations. The detectives could hear me, but I could not hear them. Sergeant Terry stated what area we would be going to. He also said that they would have a visual contact with me at all times. Sergeant Terry stated that they would send detectives into the area looking for a group of males hanging out and then drop me off close to that area. When the detectives were set up, they would have me walk into that area. A detective then fitted me with the wire under my sweatshirt and then we were ready to roll.

It was now dark out, and we drove to a staging area where I would stay out of sight until the detectives located a spot for me to be dropped off. I could hear the detectives talking on the car radio about people hanging out in certain areas. I was calm sitting in the car listening to the chatter until I heard Sergeant Terry say that there were four or five people hanging out. He gave the location and instructed the detectives to set up and then "send Rick in." The detectives set up so they could watch me, and then I was let out of the car.

I would like to tell you I was confident, but I really felt intimidated. I still had my weapon with me, and I knew that even if the detectives were watching me, it would take a little time before they would get to assist me. I pulled up my hood and walked slowly toward a group of five males. I remembered the street I was on when I worked in a zone car and traveled up and down a thousand times. Now I was walking it alone at night. As I approached this group, I noticed that one of the men had a golf club in his hand. I thought, *Oh great, I'm going to get cranked in the head with the golf club.* I thought, *This really stinks.* I thought I was going to get knocked out with the club, but the detectives would grab them after.

I was now face-to-face with the man with the club, and he asked me if I wanted to buy some crack. I told him I was good, and I now had my back to him, walking away. I thought for sure I was going to get hit in the head as I was walking away, but no, he didn't hit me. Thank you, God. I walked to the end of the street where I was picked up by the detectives, and we returned to the staging area. I waited there until the detectives spotted another group.

While I waited at the staging area, I began to pray again. I asked God if these criminals were out tonight, let the detectives locate them. I again asked God to have them approach me and rob me. This was the second time tonight I asked to get robbed. I waited at the staging area for about fifteen minutes when I heard Sergeant Terry give out another location where there were males hanging out. Once again, the detectives set up and I was dropped off. I approached the group, and nothing happened. I was picked up and taken back to the staging area. This went on for about four hours where the detectives would locate a group and have me approach. Every time, nothing happened.

I heard Sergeant Terry on the police radio say that we would try one more time, and if nothing happened, we would call it a night. Just as Sergeant Terry finished talking, I heard on the radio a detective announce that he could see a group of about ten males hanging out on a corner close to a small neighborhood store. Once again, I was dropped off down the street from the store. I turned the corner, and I could see the group of males. The store was lit up by a small outdoor light. I put my hood up and walked toward the group.

I walked like I was drunk. I again prayed the same prayer. This time felt different. I looked up and I saw that the group was walking toward me and they were talking very loudly. When I was face-to-face with the group, they surrounded me in a half circle with my back to the store. One of the males pulled out five dollars and told me to buy him cigarettes. I acted drunk, and then I saw a second male pull out a gun and demanded money. This was happening very quickly. I turned around quick and spoke into my sweatshirt. I said, "Come on, guys, he's got a gun." I forgot that the detectives were listening to everything. Suddenly, the group started running, and I didn't realize why. The detectives were responding to what they had heard, and the group saw them and realized it was the police. What a visual. Everyone was running and being pursued by the police. Everyone from the group was caught and arrested.

It turned out that everyone involved was a juvenile. The gun that was recovered was a toy. I often think about what would have happened if I would have shot that juvenile. I believed it was a real weapon. I even called it out on the radio. Today, the public isn't sympathetic to what the police perceive at the time of a critical incident. I didn't want to take the time to ask the juvenile if the gun he was using was real or a toy. He got the jump on me. I didn't want to look him in the face, because I thought if he realized that I could identify him, he might shoot me. That's a lot to think about in a fraction of a second.

The juveniles were taken to the police station and they were all booked. Their parents were contacted, and the juveniles were interviewed. During the interviews, it was revealed that the juveniles' intentions were to rob me. The juveniles were questioned about several other robberies in the area. It was the same method of operation. It was a group of males who approached elderly males and then beat and rob them. A few of the juveniles who were interviewed did admit to taking part in the previous robberies and implicated their friends.

The juveniles were charged and appeared in juvenile court in front of a magistrate. I testified against all of them. The biggest obstacle was the toy gun. The attorneys argued that since it was a toy, it shouldn't be considered a robbery. The juvenile with the gun could have been shot that night. The lawyer just wanted to help his client. I understand he was doing his job. In the long run, if there isn't a lesson learned, the same mistake will be repeated. I have watched news stories with similar circumstances. A juvenile has a toy gun and ends up dead. It's time to get rid of toy guns that are made to look like the real thing. A police officer should not have to make a life-changing decision in trying to decide if what he is looking at is a toy or the real thing.

It could be that God was watching out for that juvenile with the gun. I hope he was paying attention. I wonder if the juvenile realized what type of danger he was in. He could have been shot. Maybe someday the juveniles will realize that when they approached me and attempted to rob me, it was an answer to my prayer. I would be willing to bet that I wasn't the only one praying for these juveniles to get caught. I believe some of the victims and their family and the neighbors of the victims prayed. God just used our vice unit and me as a decoy to put a stop to these robberies. I believe it was God's will that the juveniles were caught.

I would like to tell you that I continued my career working undercover, but that wouldn't be true. I was a one and done undercover detective. Now that's something to think about. I went undercover one time and I was approached and robbed at gunpoint. I think most detectives would tell you that it's not something that happens on a regular basis.

When God is involved, anything is possible. In the Bible in Matthew 19:26, Jesus said, "With man this is impossible. But with God all things are possible." I have claimed this Bible verse for my life. I believe if it is in God's will, anything is possible. I love to pray and make requests to God, and I love waiting to see the results. I have made a lot of requests, and I would like to tell you I have seen all my prayer requests answered, but that would be a lie. I know everything is not answered immediately. Sometimes it might take years and years, but as long as I'm alive, I will continue to watch for the answers. That is why we need to pay attention, because we might miss the answers.

I believe my coworkers were starting to pay attention to me. I explained that God had answered my prayer to get robbed. I didn't want the attention on me, I wanted it on God. I started to use the police stories to witness to my friends, family, and coworkers. My hope was that they would put their trust in God. I wanted them to know that God is alive and still doing miracles.

Chapter 6

Why Change?

My career as a detective was coming to an end. I decided to take the promotional exam to become a sergeant. I had mixed emotions prior to taking the test. I was feeling secure about working a day-shift job and had made good friends in the detective bureau. God was answering prayers, and I was in a comfortable routine at work and home. I knew that if I got promoted, I would most likely go back to working the midnight shift. I hated the midnight shift. My children were older now and didn't need me as much. They were now able to drive on their own.

I studied hard for a few months prior to the test and felt like I was ready. I must admit that I was not a good student in school. I did not take a book home at any time during my four years of high school. My wife, who is a schoolteacher, wonders how I ever graduated. That's a good question. It's funny, because when I was reading the literature for the promotional exam, I realized that I was capable of understanding and retaining what I read. Now, that's truly a miracle.

I want to tell you what my prayer to God was about. I asked God that I have recall of what I studied. I realized when praying that if God wanted me to get promoted, nothing was going to stop that. If God didn't want me to get promoted, I wouldn't get promoted. It was as simple as that. I thought God would put me where he wanted me.

When the day of the test arrived, I felt confident but nervous. I had no idea how I did on the test. The results were not immediately given. The results and rankings usually took two or three months. It was a waiting game. While waiting for the results, I would get anxious and nervous at times. I wondered if God wanted me to move on to a new position, and what would he have in store for me if I moved on. I also thought that he might want me to stay right where I was. I felt comfortable in the detective bureau. I also thought that maybe I made a mistake taking the test. I thought, why would I want to disrupt my life at this time? After all these different scenarios went through my head, I knew I needed to just trust God. One thing I know, when you're confused about your life, trust God and he will give you rest. Amen to that.

The test result and the rankings came out, and I scored well enough to get promoted. I didn't score high enough to get promoted in the first class, but high enough to eventually get promoted. I knew that my life was going to change, and I wondered how I would respond to this change.

It didn't take long to figure out how my life was changing. The day of the promotion ceremony, I found out I was going to be sent to the Fourth District on midnight shift. The Fourth District was known to be the busiest district in the city. When I first started my career as a police officer, I heard that you could learn more about being a police officer at the Fourth District in a year than any other district over several years.

Police officers do not like change, and I was no different. When I arrived at the Fourth District, I immediately had to figure out how to be a sergeant. As a police officer and detective, I knew what was expected of me, but I had no idea what the responsibilities of a sergeant were. I felt like a rookie all over again. When you are a rookie police officer, you are taught by a platoon of men and women, and you are expected to grow by what you see and what you are taught while you are working. It is a slow, steady process. When you become a sergeant, you get thrown into the fire. You have thirty or forty people looking to you and watching to see if you know what you're doing. It is intimidating at first. The first week at the Fourth District, I felt like I had made a mistake, a big mistake.

I thought about several sergeants who had supervised me during my career. Police officers spoke about bosses whom they thought were good or bad. I wanted to be a good supervisor, but I also wanted to be liked. I also knew that a lot of patrol officers do not trust their boss. It really is a balancing act. I reevaluated how I thought about the sergeants I worked for when I was a patrol officer and detective.

After a few months of being a sergeant, I called Sergeant Bruce, who was my boss in the detective bureau. I wanted him to know how much I appreciated him. I apologized to him for the way I had treated him. I realized that I was hard on him at times and skeptical and most of the time without cause. I wanted him to know that now that I was a sergeant, I realized what he was trying to accomplish as my supervisor. He was always fair and kind and available to talk with. He was not only a good boss but also a kind man. I never saw him upset or raise his voice. A great example and one of a kind. Thank you again, Sergeant Bruce.

I would like to say that things got better working at the Fourth District, but they didn't until I realized what I had been doing wrong the whole time. I was trying to establish myself with the patrol officers and forgot how to bring God into my work environment. I was doing things on my own and left God out. My friend Russ always quoted Proverbs 3:5–6. It says, "Trust in the Lord with all your heart and lean not on your own understanding. In all your ways submit to him, and he will make your paths straight." I was leaning on my own understanding. Once I stopped feeling sorry for myself and started to look for God at the Fourth District, my outlook changed. When you bring God to work, it makes work exciting and fun. My advice to anyone reading this: do not leave God at home when you go to work.

I brought God to work with me, and initially I thought that God was going to solve crime again. That didn't happen with me. God had other plans at this time. I soon realized that I was supposed to tell other police officers about God. I was able to tell officers about how God had shown me miracles during my life and how he was involved in my police work. It's funny that when I had one-on-one conversations with officers about God, I learned that other officers were Christians and they would tell me about how God was active in their life. Sometimes we feel all alone because we don't talk about God to anyone. That is a trick of the devil. Don't talk about God because people will think you're nuts or a fanatic. My pastor, Brian Edwards, believes that the reason people do not talk about God is because they fear men. I now realized that I was not alone at the Fourth District. There were a lot of police officers who believed in Jesus. Whenever I had the chance, I would seek them out.

I now knew the reason I was at the Fourth District working midnights. I learned how to be a sergeant, but I was not involved directly in solving any crime. In Isaiah 55:8, God says, "For my thoughts are not your thoughts, neither are your ways my ways." God is in control of all things. I had to take "me" out of the situation and trust God. I had to learn that lesson again for me to move forward.

I can look back now when I got promoted to sergeant and see how I wasn't ready to move forward. I was not able to move forward until I learned a lesson from God. God told me to pay attention. Once I paid attention to God, he promoted me. I'm not talking about God promoting me to sergeant. I'm talking about God promoting me to my next heavenly assignment. It took me a year, and that's okay, because I changed. I not only changed jobs at the police department, but I now realize that God corrected me because I needed to change. God wanted me to look at things the way he looks at them. Thank you, Lord.

Chapter 7

The Bike Story

My time at the Fourth District was coming to an end. The police department had put out an anticipated assignment for a sergeant for the SWAT team. I thought about trying out for the team, but wasn't sure if I could make it. I knew you had to take a physical exercise test, which included a timed run and a shooting test, and then, if you made it that far, an interview. I had an idea what the SWAT team duties were. I knew they did search warrants and barricaded suspects, and when the president of the United States would visit, the team would help the Secret Service with protection. I knew it was a dangerous job. I was interested in becoming a member of the team.

I spoke to my wife about trying out for the team, and she was supportive. Once my wife gave me her support, I asked God for his support. Once again, I left it in God's hands. My prayer to God was, "If you want me to transfer to SWAT, then nothing can stop your will for me. If you don't want me to transfer to SWAT, then nothing I do can change the outcome." I was hoping that God would let me get transferred.

The day of the testing began, and I was able to pass the physical exercise part and the timed run. I also passed the shooting part of the test. The last thing I had to do was to be interviewed by the SWAT supervisors. When everything was completed, I wondered, if God allowed me to go to SWAT, what was I supposed to accomplish? I had no idea. I did know that the SWAT team had a great reputation and there were several team members who were assigned to SWAT for over twenty years. That is a lot of knowledge and experience. I wondered if there were any Christians in the unit.

It took about two months before I found out that I was picked for the job, and I also found out that they had picked another sergeant at the same time. The other sergeant picked for the job was named Dan. Dan had previously worked in SWAT when he was a patrol officer. Dan's prior experience benefitted me because he was always willing to teach me and help me in SWAT procedures. Thank you, Dan.

I had been working at the police department for about eighteen years, and once again, I felt like a rookie officer. There was so much to learn. The number one thing I learned was how to work safely. I also learned the importance of teamwork and communication. Training was very important. Every SWAT officer was expected to stay in good physical shape and be proficient in weapon training. It took me about a year to feel comfortable being the supervisor and understanding why and how we responded to certain situations. There was a reason for everything we did, and nothing was random.

The SWAT unit had a day-shift crew and an afternoon crew. The two shifts would come together one day a week to train. The unit would do around 500 search warrants a year and approximately 40 barricade suspects a year. The two shifts would come together for barricaded suspects. It was amazing to see how everyone would respond in tense, dangerous situations. They were always professional and calm under the most stressful situations. It's not easy going into a home where you have intelligence that they have weapons, dogs, and at times surveillance cameras. There were times the team would enter a home or business knowing that the person inside had already killed someone.

The men in the SWAT team were the best of the best, and I often wondered where I fit in. I knew God had put me in the unit for a reason. I had several opportunities to talk one-on-one with some of the guys about my life before Christ and how God had changed my life after I accepted Christ as my Lord and Savior. I wanted them to know. I would like to tell you that I was always a good example to the men in the unit, but that wouldn't be true. I lost my temper several times, and with that comes a feeling of guilt and regret. I would like to think that I learned a lesson each time. You will read later how God taught me a lesson about my anger.

Getting dressed for SWAT is a big deal. SWAT members wear a Kevlar helmet and a dragon-skin bulletproof vest. Some members wear Kevlar shin guards, Kevlar forearm guards, and protective glasses. All the members wore boots. SWAT also uses shields at times when entering a home or moving from location to another location. All members carry automatic handguns, and some carry a shotgun or an M-4. This protective gear gave us a sense of defense against a hostile enemy. I tell you all of this because God reminded me about what it says in the Bible about the enemy.

If you read Ephesians 6:11–18, it says,

> [P]ut on the full armor of God, so that you can take your stand against the devil's schemes. For our struggles is not against flesh and blood, but against the rulers, against the authorities, against the powers of this dark world and against the spiritual forces of evil in the heavenly realms.

Therefore, put on the full armor of God, so that when the day of evil comes, you may be able to stand your ground, and after you have done everything, to stand. Stand firm then, with the belt of truth buckled around your waist, with the breastplate of righteousness in place, and with your feet fitted with the readiness that comes from the gospel of peace. In addition to all this, take up the shield of faith, which you can extinguish all the flaming arrows of the evil one. Take the helmet of salvation and the sword of the spirit, which is the word of God. And pray in the spirit on all occasions with all kinds of prayers and request. Be alert and always keep on praying for all the Lord's people.

To me, it looks like the author of Ephesians was describing a SWAT member getting dressed for battle. God reminded me about this passage in the Bible when I would get dressed for battle.

I wanted to give you some background about SWAT before I told you about the bike story. This story is one of my favorite miracles to share. You will see that God defies all odds. He does what we believe is impossible. In Matthew

17:24–27, Jesus told Peter to go fishing and to take the first fish that he catches, open the fish's mouth, and he would find a piece of money. He then told Peter, after he finds the money, to go and pay the temple tax. What are the odds? How many fish are there? How many fish have coins in their mouths? We must have faith that God will do the impossible. He surely did the impossible with the story I'm about to tell.

My wife and I went to my mother-in-law's home for a picnic on Memorial Day. While at the picnic, my cousin Julie introduced me to her fiancé, Dave. I knew Julie was a Christian, but I didn't know what Dave believed. I knew nothing about Dave. I thought about waiting when Dave was alone so I could talk with him. I wanted to get to know him and what he believed. I was hoping to create a friendship.

I later noticed that Julie went inside the house and Dave was sitting outside alone. I approached Dave and sat with him at the table. I asked Dave how he met Julie and he said he met Julie at church. Dave then told me how his relationship evolved from friends to future husband and wife. I asked Dave where he lived, and he said about one mile from downtown Cleveland. I asked Dave how he liked living so close to downtown. Dave said he loved it because he could ride his bike to work, and it was just across a bridge which lead downtown. Dave then said he couldn't ride his bike anymore because someone had broken into his garage recently and stolen his bike. At this time, Julie called for Dave, and our conversation ended.

My wife and I stayed at the picnic for a couple more hours and then decided to leave. When we said our good-byes to Dave and Julie, I told Dave that if he wanted, I could come and pick him up at his house the next day. I explained that I would be working the afternoon shift in SWAT, and if we didn't have any search warrants to do, I could pick him up around 6:00 p.m., and we could look for his bike. He didn't know that my intention was to look for his bike and to get to know him better. I told Dave and Julie that since I had been a police officer, several kids from our neighborhood have had their bikes stolen. I let them know that I had recovered every single bike for the kids. I told them I pray and ask God to lead me to the bikes. I was bragging. I wanted Dave and Julie and anyone else present to hear what I just said so when the bike was found, they would know it was God.

I know if you're reading this right now, you're probably thinking, what's the big deal about finding a bike that was stolen? If you're helping a young kid, it's a big thing to them. This is their main source of transportation. A bike could have been a Christmas gift or a birthday present, or maybe they had worked and saved up money to buy it. I wanted the kids to know I cared, and I also wanted them to know that Jesus cared. I made sure I told them that I prayed to find their bike. They were witnesses to a miracle. Dave and Julie were also soon going to be witnesses to a miracle.

I went to work the next day at the SWAT unit and saw that we did not have any search warrants to do. I called Dave and asked him if he was still available to go and look for his bike. Dave said yes, and we made arrangements. Prior to going to Dave's home, I stopped to pray. It was a simple prayer. I asked God to lead us to the bike. I asked God if he would have the person who stole the bike ride in the area where we were patrolling.

I picked Dave up and we drove around looking for his bike. I asked Dave to describe his bike. He said it was a black Trek. I had no idea what a black Trek looked like, so I just looked for a black bike. We saw several people riding bikes, and when we got close to the rider, Dave would say, "That's not my bike." We drove around for two or three hours looking. During this time with Dave, I got to know more about him. I asked him a lot of questions. He spoke about Julie and how much he loved her. He told me about his job and his plans to go back to college. Dave also spoke about his relationship with Christ.

Dave asked me what it was like being a police officer and what a day looks like working in SWAT. I told Dave that working in SWAT was a great job. I said some days we are busy and other days a little slower. I told him that some days, we could do several search warrants across the city. I let him know that SWAT members were allowed an allotted time to exercise during the shift. I explained how on slower days, we would spend a few hours on patrol and the unit would back up zone car radio runs where a gun was mentioned. I let him know that today was a slower day and that's why we were able to look for his bike.

We did not find Dave's bike that night. I was disappointed because I had bragged to Dave that we would find his bike. I drove Dave back to his house and told him we could look again tomorrow if we didn't have search warrants to do. Dave agreed, and I told him I would call him and let him know the next afternoon. It was weird; as soon as I dropped Dave off, my lovely wife, Laura, texted me and asked if I found Dave's bike. I told her that I had just dropped Dave off and we didn't find the bike. My wife, being a considerate and kind woman, texted me back. She said, "You're losing it, old man." I had to laugh.

After I dropped Dave off, I returned to the SWAT unit. A short while later, a lieutenant from the narcotics unit came to my office and asked if our unit was available to do a search warrant. So much for a quiet slow night. I told him yes and he said he would be back in a half hour so he could brief our unit about the search warrant.

During a briefing, we review the search warrant, which is signed by a judge. The warrant describes the house and several other details. The detective whose case it is will draw a picture on a chalkboard and describe what we might expect once inside the home. We like to know how many people are inside the home, if there are weapons or dogs. The briefing is important, and the more intelligence we have the better.

We were briefed by the narcotic detective and found out that this was related to drug sales. Most of our search warrants are connected to drug sales. We completed the briefing around 10:00 p.m. and agreed on a staging location not far from the target house. We put our battle gear on and went to the staging location.

I was thinking that this warrant was going to run into overtime and I was hoping to get home in time before my wife went to bed. Little did I know that my slow day that I told Dave about earlier was about to get busy.

We met the narcotic detectives at the staging location, and were told that the target male was home and it was okay to go to the house and do the search warrant. We drove to the house, exited our vehicles, and approached the front door. The narcotic detectives exited their vehicles; they were responsible for outside cover. Their responsibility was to not let anyone inside the house once we entered and to stop anyone inside that might attempt to exit the home.

The SWAT doorman banged on the front door and announced that the police were at the door and we had a search warrant. No one from inside responded to the front door. At this time, the doorman used a ram and knocked the front door lock open. We then entered the home like we had done hundreds of times before. When I entered the home, I observed four males inside, and I immediately heard a SWAT team member state that one of the males had a gun in his waistband. I heard one of my team members give orders to the man to put his hands up where he could see them. The man with the gun was not following their orders and attempted to shoot one of the SWAT officers. At this time, the SWAT officers had no other option but to shoot this man with the gun. This man died at the scene.

A lot of thoughts go through your head when something this tragic happens. I wondered why this man didn't follow directions. We had done hundreds of search warrants where people have had guns when we entered the home. Everyone prior had followed directions. To this day, I have no idea why this man did what he did.

The police department's shooting team investigators responded to this scene, conducted their investigation, and we later went to the Justice Center for further statements. It was early morning when I arrived home. My wife was getting ready for work and had no idea why I was coming home so late. The last contact I had with her was when she had sent me a text message that said I was losing it. I rarely told my wife what I did at work unless it was unusual. I didn't want her to worry. I believe most police officers family members do not have any idea what a police officer does daily.

I told my wife what happened at the search warrant, and she asked me a thousand questions. Can you guess what her last question was? She asked me about the bike. I told her we did not recover the bike, but we were going to go and look again. I told her I was confident we were going to find it. I knew God knew exactly where it was and who had it.

I believe the bike is connected to the above story. When a police officer is involved in a shooting, other officers want to know what happened. I believe officers want to understand and learn from critical incidents. In SWAT, we would debrief all our barricade incidents. We wanted to understand what we did right and what we might have done wrong. It was always to improve our tactics.

The following days after the shooting, we had several calls to do search warrants throughout the city. The vice units would call us to do their search warrants. There is a criterion for when the vice units were to call SWAT to handle the search warrants. Most of the vice unit search warrants were handled by the vice detectives, but if the intelligence revealed weapons or a tendency for violence, SWAT should be called to do the warrants.

There is a difference the way SWAT secured a home and the way the vice units did their warrants. SWAT secured the homes much slower than vice. I believe vice experiences showed that when they would hit a house, the people inside would try to flush the drugs. Vice wanted to stop the suspects before they flushed. The officers in SWAT didn't care about the drugs, they wanted to secure a home slowly and safely. I understand the vice detective reasons for doing a lot of their warrants by themselves.

It was a few days after the shooting when SWAT received a call from Vice Sergeant Tom. Sergeant Tom wanted SWAT to execute a search warrant and asked if we could meet him at a staging location. Sergeant Tom stated that we will be briefed when we meet. We had assisted Sergeant Tom and his vice unit before, but most of his search warrants were done by his unit without SWAT.

We geared up and arrived at the staging location around 6:00 p.m. We were met by Sergeant Tom and his vice unit. Sergeant Tom explained that the drug dealer was not home yet and that he had detectives watching the house. Sergeant Tom stated that when the suspect came home, we could do the warrant. Sergeant Tom stated that we were about a block away from the house. I realized that there was nothing unusual about this warrant and I wondered why the vice unit wanted to use us.

After briefing with the vice unit, Sergeant Tom came over to our van and got inside. Sergeant Tom stated that the reason he asked us to do his search warrant was because he wanted to know what happened with the shooting earlier in the week. It's like I said earlier, I believe he wanted to learn from our shooting. There is nothing wrong with that. I briefed Sergeant Tom on what had happened during the warrant. After talking with him, he thanked us for coming to do his warrant and told us to stay safe.

We waited for about forty-five minutes for the suspect to come home. We heard one of the vice detectives who was watching the suspect's house state that the suspect had just come home and had walked into his house. At this time, Sergeant Tom broadcast on the police radio to have SWAT hit the house. We started down Lorain Avenue, driving toward the house. We then heard the vice detective who was watching the house state that the suspect had just left his house on a bike and was heading down Lorain Ave.

Sergeant Tom stated that he would grab him off his bike. At this time, I saw a male riding a bike toward us. He was approximately thirty or forty yards away from our van. I saw Sergeant Tom stop his vehicle and jump out of his car and arrest the male. I noticed that the bike that the suspect was riding was black. I didn't notice anything else.

I saw Sergeant Tom open his trunk and throw the bike in the back of his car. I thought to myself, *Be careful, that's Dave's bike.* Sergeant Tom attempted to close the trunk, but it wouldn't shut because the bike was sticking out. I again thought to myself, *Be careful, that's Dave's bike.*

After Sergeant Tom had everything under control with the suspect, we went to the suspect's house and executed the search warrant. When we completed the search warrant, I immediately went to where the bike was. Sergeant Tom had taken the bike out of his trunk and put it on the sidewalk. I looked at the bike and I saw that it was a black Trek. I also noticed that it had a round silver bell on the handlebar. I thought, Dave never mentioned that it had a girl bell on the handlebar.

The suspect was now sitting in the back of a zone car. I went over to him and opened the door. I asked him where he had gotten the bike. I was surprised what he told me. In his words, he said he got the bike from a crackhead. He had traded some crack for the bike. I told him that I was taking the bike because it was stolen. He couldn't care less. That was the least of his worries. He was under arrest for dealing drugs and his house was now being searched by the vice unit.

It was funny when I look back now. The vice unit was searching the house and there were about ten SWAT personnel outside the home. I asked the SWAT team to hang around the house because I thought this might be Dave's bike. They probably thought I was nuts because I was curious about the bike.

I called my wife and asked her to contact Dave or Julie. I wanted them to come to our location. I also wanted Dave to bring any type of ownership paperwork for the bike. About fifteen minutes later, my wife contacted me and told me that Dave and Julie were on their way.

I will never forget this day as long as I live. I remember I was outside standing with the bike talking with a few of the SWAT team members when I saw Dave and Julie drive up. Dave had his window down, and as he was pulling up he yelled out the window, "I can't believe you found my bike." I was shocked to say the least.

Dave and Julie parked the car and got out. I saw that Dave had some paperwork in his hand. Dave said it was his bike paperwork and the bike serial number. We checked the paperwork serial number with the bike serial number, and it was an exact match. This was 100 percent Dave's bike. Wow.

What had just happened? This wasn't an accident. I was looking for Dave's bike a few days earlier. I guess people could say that if I had found Dave's bike when I was actively looking, it was just good police work. Police work had nothing to do with finding the bike. I believe God directed me to this bike. God wanted to perform a miracle.

I want to show you the chain of events that led up to this miracle. Dave had his bike stolen from his garage. I met Dave for the first time on Memorial Day, and he told me about the theft of his bike. The next day, I picked Dave up and rode around looking for his bike. That same day, SWAT did a search warrant where a man died when he attempted to shoot a SWAT officer. A few days later, SWAT was called to do a search warrant for vice. I was told by Sergeant Tom that he only called us to do the warrant because he wanted to know what happened with the male that was shot.

It should be noted that search warrants are not last-second decisions. There is a lot of work and background investigation prior to getting a narcotic search warrant. Some warrants take a couple of months' investigation before a warrant can be obtained. The search warrant that we did for the vice unit was in the works probably a month or two before Dave's bike was stolen. Lastly, what are the odds that the suspect who had the bike would come home and then get on the bike and ride toward us? If the suspect did not get on the bike, I wouldn't have looked for a bike during the search warrant. We would have done the warrant and secured the house and left. God once again put the bike right in front of my face.

How do you respond to God when he uses you in a miracle? I was overwhelmed. In the Bible, in Exodus 3:5,

Moses was in God's presence at the burning bush. God said to Moses, "Do not come any closer, take off your sandals, for the place where you are standing is holy ground." I knew I was in God's presence. I knew I was standing on holy ground. God then told Moses, "I am the God of your father, the God of Abraham, the God of Isaac, and the God of Jacob." When Moses heard what God had said, he hid his face, for he was afraid to look at God. I was in awe. I felt like I should be lying prone on the ground with my face down and praising God.

I never did ask Dave and Julie how they felt about this miracle. I know Dave and Julie now refer to this miracle as the "bike story."

Chapter 8

The Apology

I wondered how the apostles and the people who witnessed the miracles of Jesus could ever go back to their lives without changing the way they lived. How do you think you would live differently if you saw Jesus heal the sick and raise the dead or control the weather? How about walking on water, or feeding thousands with several fish and a few loaves of bread?

I wish I could say I would have stopped sinning, but that wouldn't be true. How do I know this? Jesus is showing me miracles today and I still have certain sins that keep popping up in my life. I have learned several hard lessons because of my sins. I know God wants me to change. The following story is about one of my sins that took several years for me to correct.

I was working for the police department, and at that time, if you worked for the city of Cleveland, you had to live within the city boundaries. It was a residency rule. I had lived in Cleveland for almost all my life. It didn't matter to me at first, but the longer I worked as a police officer, I realized that it could be dangerous to live where I worked. There were a lot of Cleveland city employees who broke the rules by moving out of the city during this period, and when the city found out, they were terminated. I did not want to take that chance of losing my job.

I had lived in my house with my wife and kids for about ten years when my neighbor decided to sell his home. When his home sold, I wondered, who was going to be my new neighbor? It's an uneasy feeling when someone new moves next to you. I wondered if it was a younger couple or an older couple, or maybe even a single person. Did they have kids or pets? Would they take care of the home? I hoped that whoever moved in was not a party person. I was doing a lot of stinking thinking.

The day of reckoning came, and my new neighbors had moved into their home. They were a married couple who were about the same age as my wife and me. They had a young son and a teenage daughter living with them and an older daughter who was on her own. I saw that they had two small dogs.

At first impression, I felt that they were going to be good neighbors. I hate to say this, but I was judging them without first getting to know them. That wasn't fair to them. As a police officer, it was hard for me to trust anyone I first met without spending quality time with them. I also knew that I wasn't going to spend quality time with my new neighbors. I didn't want to get to close with my neighbors. I felt if something went wrong and a disagreement or argument started, it would be difficult to feel comfortable in everyday living.

I had it all planned out. I would say hello and make small talk with my neighbor. I wouldn't invite them to my house, and I would refuse politely to go to their house if invited. Hopefully, we could talk for a minute when I was outside mowing the lawn or maybe in passing on my way to work. As I look back on the way I thought, I realize that my thinking was improper. I really didn't give a friendship with my neighbor a fair chance.

What kind of Christian would think like I did? God was allowing me to see miracles and letting me be part of them, and I was worried about making a friendship with my neighbor. In the Bible, it says that Jesus was asked what the greatest commandment was in the Law. Jesus replied, "Love the Lord your God with all your heart and with all your soul and with all your mind. This is the first and greatest commandment. And the second is like it: Love your neighbor as yourself. All the law and the Prophets hang on these two commandments."

At times, I wanted to believe that I followed these two commandments, but as soon as my neighbor did something I didn't like or agree with, I immediately put up a wall. Once you put walls up, they are hard to take down. Strong walls are usually put up because of pride. In Proverbs 13:10, it says, "Where there is strife, there is pride, but wisdom is found in those who take advice." In Psalms 10:4, it says, "In his pride the wicked man does not seek him; in all his thoughts there is no room for God." I wrote about these two Bible verses on pride because they pertain to me and my thought process when I started to put up a wall against my new neighbor.

I first spoke to my new neighbor when I was outside cutting my lawn. I found out that his name was Ted and his wife's name was Gloria. We talked for about five minutes, and then I went back to cutting the lawn. I finished and went back into my house and told my wife that I had met our new neighbor. My wife wanted to know what he told me. I explained that we didn't talk long, but he seemed okay.

I wonder if Ted thought I was okay when he first met me. I was only thinking about how I felt about him, not what he thought. Our relationship stayed cordial for about two years. We would wave hello to each when we saw each other, and on occasion, we would have short conversations. I think we were comfortable as neighbors. I didn't get involved in his business, and he didn't get involved in mine. Perfect neighbor!

Everything changed with my neighbor Ted when I found out we differed on politics. Imagine that. I think I was the first person to ever get angry because of opposing political views. (I'm laughing as I'm writing.) I'm not going to write about what I believed at that time about politics, but it was different from what Ted believed. I broke my own neighborly rule when I asked Ted his political view on Cleveland's upcoming election and Ohio's governor race. This time, we didn't talk for five minutes, it was almost an hour. Ted told me his thoughts, and I told him what I thought. We were both being gentle in our conversation with each other without being insulting.

When our conversation ended, I knew I felt different about Ted. I went back inside my house and told my wife what Ted's political beliefs were. Laura couldn't care less. I knew one thing; I was going to start to put up a small wall. Ted didn't agree with me, and up goes a wall. Have you ever done that before? Do you think it would better if we could visually see the walls we put up? If I was a brick-layer, I would have put two rows of bricks starting from the ground up between me and Ted. The two rows would signify that I do not like Ted's political beliefs.

After that conversation with Ted, I felt different. When we would see each other, we would still wave to each other, but I knew the wall was there. I felt like Ted had started his own wall. You won't believe what I decided to do next.

A couple of weeks had passed since our political conversation, and I had a great idea. I went to campaign headquarters and picked up a couple of political yard signs. You know the kind of signs I'm talking about. The sign that has a name and a clever quote. I went home and cut my grass, so the front yard would look nice and freshly cut. I proudly planted my signs into the front lawn, and I just knew the signs would influence the neighborhood to think and vote like me. (Laughing again.) I couldn't wait to see how Ted would react. It didn't take long. I was leaving for work after I put the signs in the yard, and Ted was coming home at the same time. I proudly waved at Ted, and he waved back to me. I drove to work thinking that I got one over on Ted. I just want you to know, I never put up a political sign prior to this or any time after.

Can you guess what happened the next day? I was coming home from work and pulled into my driveway when I noticed that Ted had put up two political signs in his front yard. The signs were of the opponent. Now, here is when the stinking thinking comes into play. I started to get angry. I now added another row of bricks to my wall. I was now up to row three.

The silent political disagreement I was having with Ted would only end when my candidate would win the election. It's funny when I look back at that time how emotionally involved I was with the election results. I wanted to win. Wait a minute. I wanted *my candidate* to win. I would show Ted that his selection was a loser. That really means I wanted Ted to be a loser. I'm right, you're wrong; bragging rights.

Election day came, and as I was watching the results on television, I soon realized that my candidates I voted for were going to lose. I felt a little angry and a little confused. How could I face my neighbor Ted? I have heard in church and read in the Bible about respect for authority. In Romans 13:1, it says, "Everyone must submit to governing authorities. For all authority comes from God, and those in positions of authority have been placed there by God." It's funny, but I just didn't want to accept what the Bible had to say about that at this time. The Bible goes on to say in Romans 13:2, "So anyone who rebels against authority is rebelling against what God has instituted, and they will be punished."

I believe I was rebelling against what God had instituted. I think sometimes we ignore what God has to say about our lives because it means we must change. I sure wasn't ready to change yet, and do you want to know why? It's called pride. I did not want to give in to Ted, but I really knew in the back of my mind it meant submitting to God.

The day after the election, before I left for work, I took my yard signs down. I looked over at Ted's yard and at his signs with disgust. After work, I came home and noticed Ted still had his yard signs up. Ted kept his yard signs up for one week after the election was over. I now added another row of bricks to my wall. I was now on row four. Politically, I felt that those four rows of bricks would never come down. Seeing Ted and his wife daily and having to wave hello became something I hated to do. I'm not sure if they noticed, but I wanted to keep my distance from them.

Several months after the election, I noticed that Ted's oldest daughter and her husband had moved into his home. They also brought with them two dogs and lovebirds. A lot of lovebirds. With the addition of two dogs, Ted's home became loud. Ted and his family would leave the house and leave the dogs home alone. In the summer, Ted would leave his windows open when he was gone. I believe the dogs would miss Ted and his family, and as soon as they were gone the dogs would bark and howl. If they were gone for an hour, they would bark for one hour straight. If they were gone eight hours, they would bark eight hours straight. Our homes were close together, divided by a driveway. Our living room faced Ted's driveway, so when the dogs barked, the sound came into our living room. My wife and I would get frustrated and angry. This went on all summer. It was a big disruption in our lives and our downtime. I thought about telling Ted, but I didn't want to insult him. It's a hard thing to tell someone that their pets are annoying. I know some people consider pets like family.

My wife and I finally had enough of the dogs barking, so I decided when I got a chance, I would talk to Ted. I saw Ted outside in his backyard and explained what was going on when he left the house and how the dogs would bark when he was gone. Ted apologized, but he didn't offer a solution. I would have to wait and see if he would leave the dogs alone again and would they bark.

It didn't take long for us to realize that Ted did not remedy my complaint. It had been less than a week. I was at work when I received a call from my wife. My wife said that Ted and his family had left their house, and as soon as they left, the dogs started barking again. My wife said the dogs were barking nonstop for several hours. I could hear the dogs over the phone. I could also hear the frustration in my wife's voice. My wife is a very tolerant person and doesn't get upset easily. She said she wanted to call the police and make a noise complaint. I asked her not to call the police and told her to wait until I got home.

I got off work about an hour later, and when I arrived home, I noticed the dogs were not barking, and Ted and his family were back at home. I went inside my house and talked with my wife. She said she saw Ted come home and get out of his car. My wife said she opened the window and told him the dogs were barking nonstop. I asked her how he responded. She said he looked confused and didn't say anything. She believed that Ted had been drinking. My wife and I then spent the next half hour complaining to each other about our neighbor. Can you guess what we did next?

If you guessed that I added another row of bricks to my wall, you would be right. I was now on row five. This row was different. My wife helped build this row. It's nice when you have someone helping you build walls. It validates what you are feeling. It makes your wall stronger. It's also a trick of the devil. The Bible says in Peter 5:8, "Be sober minded; be watchful. Your adversary the devil prowls around like a roaring lion, seeking someone to devour." I wasn't paying attention to what God had to say about this situation. In James 4:7, the Bible says, "Submit yourselves therefore to God. Resist the devil and he will flee from you." I wasn't resisting anything. I was now ready for war, and it wasn't God supplying the ammo.

I think Ted was beginning to get the message that our relationship as neighbors was getting strained. When I saw Ted outside, I would not wave to him unless he waved to me first. I tried to ignore him as much as possible. I felt if he didn't care about us, I sure didn't care about him.

The dogs continued to bark when Ted and his family left them alone in the house. This went on for over a year. I also noticed that when I would cut my lawn in the back yard, I would step on dog feces. Ted's backyard and my backyard were not separated by a fence. The backyards were about a hundred yards long. I told my wife I was cutting the grass and I stepped in dog feces. She told me that she saw four of Ted's dogs running around in our yard and they probably used our yard as their bathroom. I felt that Ted was disrespecting us by allowing his dogs to use my yard and not clean up after the dogs.

A week had passed since I had last cut the grass. I noticed that Ted's dogs once again had used my yard to go to the bathroom. There were several piles of dog feces in one area of my lawn. This incident made me angry. I immediately went to Ted's house and complained. I asked Ted if he would stop letting his dogs loose in my yard. I explained that I had stepped in dog feces while cutting my lawn. Ted apologized and told me it wouldn't happen again, and he would clean up the mess. Ted sent his son to clean up the mess. This was the second time that I had complained to Ted about his dogs, but it wasn't the last time.

Two weeks had passed since I had complained to Ted about his dogs. I was looking out my back window, and guess what I saw? Ted's four dogs were in my yard and going to the bathroom. I didn't see Ted or anyone from his family with the dogs. The dogs were let out of the house, and when they wanted the dogs to come back, they yelled for them.

I now knew why the dogs used my yard. There was no one to direct them. I thought, why would they let the dogs out without someone being with them? I was extremely angry and I was going to let Ted know what I thought.

I went to Ted's back door and knocked. When Ted answered the door, I immediately started to yell at Ted. I told him to keep his dogs out of my yard and that I was sick of stepping in dog crap. Ted told me to stop yelling at him. I didn't stop yelling and I probably was verbally out of control. I left his house and went home and told my wife what had just happened. My wife and I were both upset. She told me she heard me yelling at Ted from inside the house. Oh well, the wall was now completed, and nothing was going to bring it down.

I made a big announcement to my wife the day after that. I told my wife we are putting the house up for sale and moving out of the City of Cleveland. I felt I could not live peacefully next to Ted. My wife asked me about the residency rule and if I would get terminated if the City of Cleveland found out that we had moved out of the city. We discussed the positive impact on our lives and the negative impact. The positive for me was getting away from Ted, and the negative was being fired from my job. We were just going to have to roll the dice and take that risk.

Do you remember in 1969 when Neil Armstrong and Buzz Aldrin put the United States flag on the moon? It was a proud moment in history. Well, I put a "for sale" sign in my front yard the day after I yelled at Ted. It was a very proud moment for me. I wanted to show Ted how much I disliked him. He would have to know he was the cause of my wife and I moving. Now all I had to do was to sit back and wait for the offers to come in.

I would like to tell you that my house sold right away. It didn't. I had my house up for sale for about six months and only had two people come and look at the house. This was unusual for the area. What I didn't realize at that time was the housing market prices had peaked and now the housing market was at the beginning of the crash. My wife told me she believed God was not going to let us sell our home until I apologized to Ted. Yeah, right, like that was going to happen. I put that thought way in the back of my head.

I took the "for sale" sign down after six months and told my wife that we will not be moving at this time. Even though the house didn't sell, I felt relieved, because I didn't want to go to work and live a lie about where I was living.

When I took the sign down, I felt defeated. I wanted to teach Ted a lesson. I felt a little embarrassed that I couldn't sell our house. My wall was fully built, and when I saw Ted or his family, we would just look at each other, but no waving or talking. Awkward would be an understatement. Even though we were not moving, I felt Ted and his family had understood the message. That was wishful thinking on my part.

Once I took our house off the market, it seemed that things got worse with Ted. The dogs continued to bark when Ted and his family left the house. Ted also had company over every weekend. The company would stay late and at times got loud outside my window. Ted and his family were raising lovebirds and would take their cages and leave them outside during the day. I would notice several birds perched on my deck fence every day watching the lovebirds. I also saw that they were leaving bird mess all over my deck. What I didn't know was they were sitting there and waiting for the lovebirds' food to fall on the ground, so they could eat it. Every day, I had to clean up a lot of bird poop on my deck. I knew Ted's lovebirds were attracting the birds. I was angry, and it seemed that Ted couldn't care less. I felt like I couldn't get any peace while at my home. That's a sick feeling. I didn't know what to do. It had been almost a year since I had taken our house off the market for sale.

I started to dislike animals, especially birds and dogs. I thought I couldn't enjoy nature because of Ted. I could tell my wife was not happy with what was going on. Ted and his family dominated our conversation and we would spend hours discussing how inconsiderate they were. I remember going on vacation and having a great time and then dreading coming back home. My wife and I talked, and we decided to once again put our house up for sale. Maybe this time we would have better luck.

I put the "for sale" sign in the front yard, and it wasn't as exciting as the first time. I didn't know what to expect. We hired a different realty company. We wanted someone with a different strategy to present our house. Laura and I did pray and asked God if he would send someone to buy our house. Laura again told me that she believed I should apologize to Ted. Laura said she believed God wouldn't let us sell the house until I apologized. This time it sank in, and I thought about what she told me. I knew she was right, but I didn't want to give in to Ted. I felt like he should apologize to me. My wall was way too high to apologize.

The housing market crash was now in total collapse. To make things worse, the Ohio Supreme Court upheld a 2006 state law that enforced residency. What that ruling meant for me was I could now move out of the City of Cleveland legally. You would think that the ruling would have made me happy. I was happy and disappointed at the same time. The reason I was disappointed was that when residency was enforced, all city workers had to live in the city. When a new employee came to work for the city, they had to buy a home within the city limits. There was a built-in group of buyers, which made it easier to sell your home. I now lost this group of buyers. I knew this ruling was going to affect the sale of our home.

My wife and I started to look for houses to buy outside the city. Every weekend, we would attend open houses. We needed to be ready to buy a house just in case we had an offer to buy our home. It was weird. We knew the market was slow and we would keep an eye out for the homes that we liked and ride by the home a month later and notice that the house was sold, or a sale was pending. I wondered, why not my house? Why was I having such a hard time selling my house? I was lucky to have people come view the home during an open house. What really upset me was homes on my street and in my neighborhood would go up for sale, and eventually, they all sold. I compared the houses in my neighborhood and view them during an open house. The home prices and the overall appearance were similar. Some of the homes that were similar were not as nice as my home.

Laura and I would discuss why these homes sold and why not ours. Laura again would say she thought God wanted me to apologize to Ted. I knew she was probably right, but I hoped she was wrong. I felt I had gone too far with my anger to apologize, and my pride had got the best of me. Every time Laura told me I should apologize, I also heard God tell me to apologize. I would try to put that thought out of my head. In the Bible, in Proverbs 16:5, it says, "Everyone proud in heart is an abomination to the Lord; he will not go unpunished." I knew I needed to check myself and do it soon.

Another year had passed, and we still did not sell our home. I again took the "for sale" sign down, and I would like to tell you that things got better with my neighbor Ted. That would be a lie. I felt things were getting worse. I believe Ted felt the same way.

One day, I came home from work and noticed that Ted had put up a wood fence, and it now separated our backyards. I was happy about the fence and I was glad it was going to keep Ted's dogs out of my yard. I also thought that it was going to help with privacy. I could now sit in my backyard and not have to see my neighbors. You know, it's funny I had thought that maybe Ted would one day put his house up for sale to get away from me. I now realized he was staying put. Ted now had his wall, but his was a physical wall and mine was a mental wall.

Now that Ted had put up his wall, I could not see what was going on next door, but I could still hear. Ted would still entertain, at times past midnight. Laura and I both worked days and had to get up early. We still heard the dogs barking when they left them alone. There were several other things that Ted and his family would do that were annoying. It's funny, when you are angry with someone, you notice every little thing, so you can justify your anger, and that's what I was doing. I now thought that Ted believed that we were attempting to move, and he didn't care how his lifestyle affected us, because we were eventually leaving.

It was around six months since Ted had put up his wall separating our backyards. I again spoke to my wife about putting the house up for sale for the third time. It was early spring, and we both agreed. I think it's important to note that my wife and I prayed almost every day for our house to sell. We would ask God to send someone to look at our house and make an offer. God knows where every person in the world is looking to buy a house, and we were asking for just one person for God to send. I wondered if our home would ever sell. I thought maybe God wanted us to stay to accomplish something in our neighborhood.

It was early in spring, and Laura and I hired a new realtor. Her name was Caroline. We saw her on a local television show. We thought, if she could sell homes on television, she must be good. She offered a new and fresh strategy. She gave us some staging tips and took professional photos of our home. She put the "for sale" sign in the front yard, and we felt confident that she would be able to sell our home.

I decided to spruce up the front yard for curb appeal. I wanted it to look nice, so I tore out the lawn and planted new seed. I then staked the outline of the lawn with rope to keep people from walking on the lawn until the new lawn had grown in. When I completed staking the lawn, Ted came out of his house and started talking to me. This surprised me, because we had not spoken to each other for a while. For a minute, I thought that maybe Ted was going to apologize to me. No, that didn't happen.

Ted wanted to warn me that he was going to get a new cement driveway in a week. He used the word *warn*. He said that since I had planted a new lawn, he was worried that the workers might step onto the newly planted lawn and he didn't want me to get upset. I thought to myself that Ted was finally learning about being courteous to me. I told Ted thanks for the warning. I explained that I had put the rope up and the workers should be able to put the new drive in without stepping on the new seed.

I finished the lawn and went inside the house, and I received a phone call from our realtor. Caroline told me she had a couple that wanted to look at our house. Caroline asked if she could show the house, and we agreed on a time, so we could prepare the house to be shown. This couple were the first people Caroline brought to see our home.

Laura and I had been through this many times before. We would clean up and stage the house. We had it down to a science. We would vacuum the house and declutter as much as possible. We would try to make the home look like a model home inside. We then would leave the house a half hour before the viewing and come back a couple hours later. We always had high hopes. We wondered if this would be the time that someone would want to make a bid on our house. Laura and I also wondered if a prospective buyer saw our neighbor Ted and his family with his dogs and his lovebirds and decided not to bid on the house because of the dogs and birds. At times, I felt guilty about selling my home to someone else because of my neighbors. Right now, I didn't have to worry about that guilt, because I wasn't getting any bids.

The realtor showed our house, and Laura and I returned to our home and waited for feedback from Caroline. Caroline called us and explained that the couple who she showed our home to did like our home, but they had several other homes scheduled to look at. That response was common to Laura and me. We came to expect rejection.

One week had gone by since I had planted the lawn and our realtor had shown our house. The lawn was starting to grow in very nicely. I went outside early and watered the lawn. I finished watering and went back inside. About an hour later, I heard noise at the front of the house. It was Ted and a couple of men. I had forgot about Ted putting a new concrete driveway in. I thought it was bad timing on Ted's part because I had just put a new lawn in. I knew it was going to make the job difficult. I was glad that I had roped off the yard, and I figured the workers would respect the newly planted lawn. Boy, was I wrong.

I watched the workers for about an hour from my living room window. It appeared that they initially tried not to step onto my lawn. I then saw the men standing on my lawn working on the driveway I could see that the new lawn was being ruined. I went outside and spoke to the workers and explained that the lawn had been planted one week ago and by standing on the lawn they were going to kill the new grass. The workers apologized and said they would try to be careful.

I went back into my house, and at that time I received a telephone call from Caroline, my realtor. Caroline asked me if she could show the house that day around 1:00 p.m. This was now the second couple to look at our house in a week. I told Caroline that would work for us. I also told her that it might be a little noisy because my neighbor was putting a new driveway in. I told Laura about showing the house, and we once again prepared by cleaning and staging the house.

When we completed cleaning the house, I once again checked to see if the cement workers were honoring my request not to stand on my lawn. What I saw were two workers standing on my lawn finishing fresh cement with a float. I saw that my lawn was flattened. Seeing this, I became angry and told my wife I was going outside to speak to them.

When I went outside, I saw that Ted was outside monitoring the workers. I would like to say that I was calm, but that would be a lie. I totally lost my temper and started to yell at Ted and the workers. I called him inconsiderate and rude. I told him I have people coming to look at my house and he was ruining the look of my front yard. Ted explained that they were trying to be careful, but it was impossible to finish the cement without standing on my lawn. I yelled so loud at Ted that when I came back inside the house, my voice was hoarse. My wife said she heard my yelling inside our house. I'm sure my neighbors heard my yelling from inside their houses. I was embarrassed how I acted, but felt like I had a right to express my feelings.

Laura and I left the house so our realtor could show the home. I was still upset and venting to Laura. When Laura and I left the house when someone wanted to look at it, we would always say a prayer together. We would always ask God, *please let this be the couple wanting to buy our house.* This time, we didn't pray. I knew why I didn't want to pray. I had just lost my temper, and everyone saw or heard. I'm sure Laura felt the same way. I knew I had sinned, and I didn't want to ask God for help because I felt God would want me to reconcile with my neighbor. Currently, I wasn't ready for that.

A couple hours went by, and we returned home and again waited to hear from Caroline. I saw that the cement truck and the workers were gone, and the drive was done. I also noticed that the cement workers had raked the lawn and the grass was sticking straight up again. I was glad they did that, and it calmed me down a little bit.

I usually waited for my realtor to call me after a showing, but this time I called her. I wanted to know right away, especially since I had just blown up at Ted. I was hoping for good news. I spoke to Caroline, and she explained that the couple liked the house, but they decided to buy a different house they had looked at prior. I felt like someone punched me in the gut. I told my wife what Caroline had said, and she was disappointed.

Laura and I then had a conversation about me yelling at Ted. Laura told me that she believed that God was not going to let us sell our home until I apologized. I then went over all the reasons that I shouldn't apologize. At the end of our conversation, I felt convicted, but I didn't tell Laura. I thought about what Laura said for the rest of the day, even when I slept. I knew my wife was right.

It had been close to three years when I first put our house up for sale. During that time, I had attended church on Sunday and Thursday, and even attended Bible study on Saturday. I had heard sermons about forgiveness and holding grudges. When I listened to these sermons, I knew the Holy Spirit was speaking to me, but I didn't want to admit it. I was hiding from the truth. I was hoping that God was going to let me get away with my sin and let me sell my house. I reasoned that Ted was making me act a certain way, and if I got away from Ted I would act differently. I thought God would understand my reasoning. My way was to run away, and God's way was to stay and work it out. I was not paying attention for the past three years. I knew it was time for me to change and start paying attention. I knew I had to apologize. I went to bed with the intention of apologizing to Ted the next day. Oh boy!

The next day, I got up and immediately thought about Ted and how I should approach him. I started to get anxious and nervous. My plan was to wait until I saw him outside and then apologize. Then I thought, *what if I don't see him outside today?* I didn't want to wait another day, because the longer I waited, the harder it was going to be for me to apologize. I might back out if I didn't see him that day. I went over in my head several times what I wanted to say to Ted. I knew I didn't want to apologize; I wanted to have an excuse for my actions. I didn't want to say that I got angry because of anything Ted or his family had done. I wanted to move on and hope that Ted would accept my apology.

In the Bible in Ephesians 4:32, it says to be kind to each other, sympathetic, forgiving each other as God has forgiven you through Christ. In 1 John 1:9, it says, if we confess our sins, he is faithful and just to forgive us our sins and to cleanse us from all unrighteousness. I knew I needed cleansing and forgiveness. I knew I had to ask God and Ted for forgiveness. Today was the day.

I waited in my living room, looking out the front window, waiting for Ted to come out of his house. I knew he would have to come out the front door, because he had parked his car in the street when he was getting his driveway replaced. I sat wondering how Ted was going to react when I approached him. I didn't have to wait too long before Ted came out of his house.

I thought, *This is it, just go and do it. Don't even think about it.* I immediately went out my front door and approached Ted. He didn't see me coming toward him. To get his attention, I just called his name in a normal tone of voice. I couldn't believe it, but Ted jumped like he was shell-shocked. I'm sure he thought I was going to yell at him again. His posture was very defensive. I knew my behavior toward Ted the past few years had affected him.

I immediately told Ted that I wanted to apologize to him for the way I've been treating him, and I was sorry for yelling at him and disrespecting him. Ted responded by telling me he was sorry. I explained to Ted that everything that was going on between us was my fault and I could have responded differently, and it wasn't his fault. Ted and I shook hands, and I again told him I was sorry.

What happened next really floored me. Ted told me that he had been praying about our situation, asking that it get resolved. When Ted told me that, I was overwhelmed with guilt. I told Ted I had been praying also. I left Ted and went back into my house.

I sat down in my living room and thought about what had just took place. I was relieved it was over. I thought that my apology was easier to do then I thought. I was glad to let all that baggage with Ted go. It was like a huge burden was lifted off me. It's hard to stay angry for a long period of time, especially when you must see that person day after day. The anger eats away at you slowly until there is nothing left but hatred. I was happy that I now got rid of my grudge and I could live in my home in peace. I now wondered how Ted and his family felt living next to me these past few years. I always felt like I was the victim, but I now realized that Ted and his family were the victims of my attacks.

Ted told me that he was praying, and that kind of freaked me out. When we were going through this with Ted and his family, my wife and I would pray and ask God for a resolution. Our answer to prayer would have been to move. I don't know what Ted was praying to God about, but I think it was about me. I knew there were people who have prayed for me throughout my life, but I didn't realize that people could be praying about me because of conflict with them. I knew that I now had to pay attention to what I just learned. God and Ted had just taught me a great lesson.

I started to think about other people with whom I had unresolved arguments, and my sister Sandy immediately came to mind. We had a bad argument a couple of years earlier and had rarely spoken to each other. I figured that I had just apologized to Ted, so I might as well apologize to my sister. I was on an apology high. I wanted to get rid of all the baggage that I carried for the past few years.

I called my sister and told her I wanted to apologize for the way I spoke to her during our argument. I explained that I was out of line and asked her for forgiveness. She was very gracious and forgiving. She asked me, what was the reason I wanted to apologize now? I didn't want to tell her about Ted, so I told her it was just time. We spoke for ten minutes, and when I got off the phone, I felt exhausted. Two apologies in one day had worn me out. I lay down on the couch and fell asleep. I was asleep for approximately fifteen minutes, but it felt like a couple of hours. I was awakened by the telephone ringing.

I answered the phone, and on the other end was my realtor Caroline. She told me that the people who had looked at our house a week ago wanted to purchase our home and submitted a bid to buy. I was shocked and was pretty much speechless. Caroline said she would contact me later in the day when she was able to review the bid. I told Caroline thank you and got off the phone.

I was sitting on my couch thinking about what had just happened. I wasn't sure if I was dreaming during my nap that my house was sold. I think it really happened. My head was a little foggy. I made a phone call to my wife, who had been shopping. I told her that I think someone put a bid on our house. Laura said, "What do you mean, you think someone put a bid?" I told her I was taking a nap and I got a phone call from Caroline, but I was half asleep when I answered. My wife said she was done shopping and she would be home shortly.

Laura came home, and she wanted to know what happened when she was gone. I told her that I apologized to Ted. She wanted to know, word for word, what was said. She wanted to know how Ted reacted to my apology. When I was done explaining what happened with Ted, she wanted to know what happened with my sister Sandy. I could see she was glad that I apologized. Laura then questioned me about the bid on our house. I told her that it was about fifteen minutes after I apologized that I got the call from our realtor Caroline. Then I heard the words that every man hears from his wife at one time or another.

"I told you! I told you God would not let us sell our house until you apologized." I have to say that my wife did tell me that in a loving, caring tone. Now, I don't really like the words *I told you so*, but this time it was like music to my ears. My wife for the past three years had told me several times that God wanted me to apologize. I told my wife that she was right. Maybe that was music to her ears. I know one thing; we were both excited and happy that we had a bid on our house.

Laura and I had a conversation on how God was involved in the sale of our home. We knew we had seen another miracle. We had our house up for sale for three years without one offer to buy. Laura had told me to apologize to Ted, and I refused. It was really God telling me to apologize to Ted, and I refused. Three years of pride and being stubborn. Three years of anger on my part. Three years of ignoring the truth. Three years of disobedience. Once I was obedient to God and apologized, I had a bid on my house.

God was teaching me a lesson. If I didn't pay attention, it would happen again. What was the lesson I needed to learn? God wants us to be obedient. He knows what is best for us. I was professing to be a follower of Jesus, and I was not acting like it. The Bible says in John 14:15, "If you love me, you will keep my commandments." I do love God, but I wasn't following the examples of Jesus. I also know that I wasn't trusting God 100 percent. God told me to apologize, and I didn't think that was such a good idea. I could surely justify in my own mind why I should not apologize.

There are many examples in the Bible about trusting God. I believed all of them, and God always kept his word to those who trusted him.

One of my favorite stories in the Bible about trusting God is in Joshua 6:1–27. The story is about the city of Jericho. It says in the Bible that the gates of Jericho were securely barred because of the Israelites. No one went out and no one came in. Then the Lord said to Joshua, "See, I have delivered Jericho into your hands, along with its king and its fighting men. March around the city once with all the armed men. Do this for six days. Have seven priests carry trumpets of ram's horns in front of the ark. On the seventh day, march around the city seven times, with the priest blowing the trumpets. When you hear them sound a long blast on the trumpets, have the whole army give a loud shout; then the wall of the city will collapse, and the army will go up, everyone straight in."

Guess what happened? They did exactly what God had told them, and the walls collapsed, and the soldiers went straight in and took the city.

When I worked in SWAT, we had numerous times when someone had committed a crime and would barricade themselves in a home. I wonder how my supervisors would have reacted if I suggested we march around the house and blow trumpets and shout.

My pastor, Brian Edwards, has given several sermons on fear of man. He believes that one of the reasons we do not profess God is because we fear what man might say or think about us. For me, that was true with Ted. I was afraid that Ted would find me weak and take advantage of our situation. The funny thing about apologizing to Ted was I felt stronger after the apology. I knew when I apologized that God was for me. He didn't say if I was right or wrong on how I acted towards Ted, but I believe God was teaching me a lesson. I needed to be obedient to his word and not fear man.

Our house did sell, and my wife and I were able to find a nice home. We were happy to move, and I was extremely happy that I left the neighborhood on a good note. I was glad that I didn't leave any negative baggage behind. I didn't know how Ted felt about me leaving. I believe now that it's better to repair a relationship than to blow it up completely. My good friend Fred once told me that it was better to eat crow when it is warm than it is to eat crow cold.

The lesson I learned about arguing was to try not to argue. If you argue and lose your temper, try to apologize as soon as possible. It doesn't matter who is right or wrong. If your wife advises you to apologize, she is probably right. The most important point to remember is, do not fear man, and when God tells you to apologize, do it immediately. We must pay attention, especially to God.

Chapter 9

What I Wanted and What I Got

I had been working in the detective bureau for several years. I enjoyed doing investigations for most of the time in the bureau. A typical day consisted of following up on felony crimes. Police officers would respond to a crime scene and make a crime report, and at times, the officers would make an arrest.

When an officer made an arrest, it was necessary to give the case immediate attention. The supervisor would assign the arrest case to a detective, and it was the detective's responsibility to charge or release the person arrested. If you were going to charge someone with the crime, it was necessary for the victim to sign a complaint form and for the detective to take a victim statement. If there were witnesses, it was necessary to take witness statements. The detective would also need to collect any crime scene photographs, fingerprints, or DNA. If a gun was used, it was necessary to get the gun test-fired to see if it was operational. If you showed a photo lineup, everyone in the lineup should look similar. It was also necessary to view any property that might have been collected as evidence. Background checks were also needed on anyone who was arrested.

Believe me when I tell you, if you miss any step during an investigation, it will be pointed out by a defense attorney during a trial. Most of the time, when a crime is initially investigated by the police officers at the scene, it is their responsibility to have the Scientific Investigation Unit (SIU) respond to the scene. The SIU is probably one of the most important units in the police department. Thousands of crimes have been solved because of the evidence that they collect at the scene of a crime. Attorneys will usually zero in on how evidence was collected.

When a detective completes his investigation, it needs to be transcribed into a hard copy, and the steps of the investigation are spelled out. The hard copy, known as the grand jury packet, is submitted to a prosecutor. The prosecutor reviews the grand jury packet, and then sets a date for the detective to appear and testify in front of the grand jury. Once the detective testifies, the jury comes back with an initial true bill or no bill. If it is a true bill, it will be set for trial.

It was not unusual for the detectives, who worked afternoon shifts, to be at the grand jury testifying in the morning on two or three cases, and then appear for a trial, and then go back to work for their scheduled tour of duty, and waiting for them was a fresh new arrest case. The detectives I worked with would receive between 150 and 200 cases in a year. To say the least, there was not a lot of downtime, and for me, I was starting to get burned out after several years. I felt like I was never off from work, and I was constantly thinking about cases.

I was thinking about a change of jobs within the police department, and if a job came open with different challenges, I was going to consider leaving the detective bureau. I was hoping to get a job working with my old zone car partner, Joe D. Joe and I had worked together in a zone car for a few years, and we had a lot of fun working together. Joe is probably one of the best police officers I know. I trusted him 100 percent. The most important thing about being a police officer is having a good partner. I know you have heard this before, but you probably know more about your partner than his wife does. You spend eight hours working together riding in a zone car, so there is a lot of personal conversations. I wanted to renew that relationship with Joe and hopefully work together again.

My opportunity to work with Joe D. came when a bid to work in the strike force was posted. Joe was already working in the strike force. There were two detective positions available. The strike force worked undercover wearing civilian clothes. There were a lot of good things about this unit. If there were a lot of burglaries or robberies in an area, the strike force would saturate the area, driving undercover vehicles, and attempt to respond to a crime in progress. The strike force did not have to respond to police radio calls, so they could stay focused in the area. If the strike force detectives made an arrest, they would handle the case from start to finish. You would live or die by your own investigation. I liked the idea of being responsible for my own work, and I liked the idea of working with Joe again. This job was perfect for us.

I spoke with Joe and told him I was going to put in for the job. I asked if we got a chance, would he want to work again together? Joe said he would like that, and that was our plan. Now the only thing left to do was to get the job.

In the police department, there are a couple different ways to get transferred. The first way to get transferred to a unit is by seniority. A seniority transfer means that if you have the most time on the department and you put in for the job, you will get the job. There is good and bad about a police officer getting a job because of seniority. In the police department, there is a lot of who you know or who you are related to. If you don't know anyone or aren't related to anyone, then getting transferred to a unit by seniority is good.

The bad thing about seniority getting a job is the officer might not have the experience needed to perform at a high level. A police officer who worked in a zone car for twenty-five years might have a problem going to a homicide unit as a seniority pick. I believe there is a learning curve going from a zone car to an investigative unit like homicide. It takes about a year to learn the paperwork and the collection of evidence and the ability to testify in court about your investigation. It's probably not the best for the victim and their families to be learning basic detective skills while investigating homicides.

There is usually a progression from working a zone car to a detective bureau. Most of the detectives picked for homicide or similar units are usually chosen from detective bureaus. Seniority picks can skip a detective bureau and go from working in a zone car to homicide. There have been times in the police department when officers did go from working a zone car to homicide, learned the job quickly, and became excellent investigators.

The second way to get transferred is to be picked by the ranking supervisor of the unit, or, in some transfers, the Chief of Police will make the picks. There can be a lot of hard feelings when an officer gets picked for a job when the officer being picked doesn't have much time on the job. If an officer has three years on the job and gets selected over an officer who has ten or more years on the job, a lot of officers take notice. The police union attempted to make it fair for all the officers involved and they negotiated with the City of Cleveland. The ruling stated that for transferring to a unit, you must have one seniority, then one chief's pick, and then seniority, then chief's pick, and so on. If a job opening came up that needed more than one police officer, the unit would get at least one seniority officer and one officer who was a pick. The senior officer could have thirty years on the job and the pick officer could have three. That is a huge difference in experience.

The third way to get transferred to a unit is to ask God. I knew if God wanted me to move, then nothing could stop it. I also knew if God didn't want me to transfer, then there was nothing, I could do to change that. I was hoping that God would let me go. I wondered if there was any reason God would say no.

I prepared my typewritten request to be transferred to the strike force. I put all the required information about myself. This information included my work history and my date of seniority. During my career, I have seen transfer bids that were two lines long and then others that were several pages long. I wasn't sure which was better, the short or the longer. If you were the seniority officer, it didn't matter about your history, because you were getting the job no matter what. It was important to write about your police history and accomplishments if you were going to be compared and chosen from a group of officers. I decided to write one page.

It's funny to think now about what I had written on the bid. I wrote a serious resume, but I really wanted to write the truth. The truth would have sounded something like this: "I respectfully request to be transferred to the strike force. My reason for this request is so I can work with my partner, Joe D., again. We work well together, and I trust him 100 percent, and we have a lot of fun. When I work with Joe, the time goes by quickly. We both know how each other will react in stressful situations. I know Joe's family, and he knows my family. Most importantly, I want to continue to witness to Joe about God. We had many conversations about God while working together and I always enjoyed them."

When I finished the paperwork for the bid, I submitted it to my commanding officer. It was now official, and almost immediately, the rumors started. Police officers are notorious for starting rumors. Officers would approach me and tell me of other officers who were also putting in for the strike force. I was hoping that I would be the seniority pick. I soon learned that another officer with more time was also going to type for the unit. What that meant for me was I was going to have to be the pick to get into the unit.

The strike force bid was available to anyone in the district and stayed open for bids for two weeks. At the end of the two weeks, a list of applicants was given to the commanding officer for review. After hearing all the rumors of who was putting in for the strike force, there was now an official list of candidates. When I looked at the list, I noticed two things. I was the second in seniority, and my friend Mike had also typed for the unit. Mike worked with Joe, and I and was the third person who worked on the zone car with us. Joe and I trained Mike when he was a rookie. Mike was a good police officer, and I knew he would make a good detective.

Now that I saw who the candidates were, I started to compare myself with them. I know it's arrogant to compare, but I did compare my experiences with the others. I felt I was more qualified and should be the pick for the strike force. Once I compared, I felt confident. To reinforce my thoughts, I had a lot of friends tell me that I should get picked for the job. They also asked if I was going to work with Joe D. again.

Did you notice how many times I said "I" in the previous paragraph? In the Bible, in Philippians 2:3, it says, "Do nothing from rivalry or conceit, but in humility count others more significant than yourselves." My initial mindset was to be humble when I thought I was going to get the job because of seniority. Now that seniority was not an option, I had to compete with several other officers. Instead of trusting God and paying attention to Philippians 2:3, I lost humility really quick and started a silent rivalry. I also did not count the other officers more significant then myself.

Pride now entered my thought process. I wondered how it would look if I didn't get picked for the job. I also wondered how I would react if Mike got the job over me. I was doing a lot of stinking thinking. Mike had worked with Joe D. on the car, and I wondered, if he got the job, would Mike work with Joe? Would I get mad at Mike if he got the job?

I knew the decision was out of my hands, and I asked God for a calm and peace during this process. I also asked God, if it was in his will to let me go to the strike force. I believed that God had watched out for me during my police career and he would watch out for me now. I didn't see any reason why not.

There is a process that takes place once a bid is posted and closed. The supervisor will review all the requests and check what experience each candidate has. The supervisor would then make appointments with each candidate for an interview. I knew the interview would be important and looked forward to it. I believed I would do well in an interview for the strike force. I also had a slight advantage because I had worked a six-month detail in the strike force a few years prior, and my zone car partner Joe D. was already in the unit.

I was waiting to hear from the strike force supervisor about scheduling an interview. I approached my lieutenant and asked if he knew when the interviews were going to start. The lieutenant told me he didn't know. What he told me next shocked me. He told me that I was going to be the pick to go to the strike force.

You would think that I would have been happy to hear that news, but I wasn't. In the police department, I had heard and saw a lot of weird things when it came to police officers getting transferred to specialized units. There were a lot of last-minute changes that took place while waiting for the transfer process. There were several instances when a police officer was told he was going to be transferred to a unit, and at the last minute it all changed and the position went to someone else. To me, it was the kiss of death to be told I was going to be transferred. There is a joke in the police department about transferring. Most officers will say they won't believe it unless it is written on paper and they are in the unit. I felt the same way.

Being told I was going to the strike force made me feel uneasy. I felt like the process was rigged and I didn't have to sell myself during the interview. I felt bad for the other candidates knowing that however they interviewed it didn't matter, because I was the pick. Over the course of my career, I had heard about officers getting picked for jobs prior to interviewing all the candidates. I didn't like it then and I didn't like it now. I had no problem competing for the job, and I didn't like knowing prior to the interview. I just wanted a fair shot.

Well, I didn't have to worry about the interview, because the supervisor didn't interview any of the officers. That was a little unusual, and I wondered why there was no face-to-face with the supervisor. The supervisor would rely strictly on the officers' written resumes.

The bid process was completed, and now all I had to do was wait for it to be announced and finalized on paper. I knew it could be as soon as a week, and sometimes it took months. I hoped it was sooner than later. While waiting, I heard a lot of rumors. Some of the rumors were positive about me getting transferred to the strike force. I heard from officers who supposedly had inside scoop. I also talked with officers who said I wasn't going to be picked because the strike force supervisor didn't like me. I wondered how they would know that the supervisor didn't like me. I wondered if the supervisor said something negative about me to another officer. I found this to be unusual, because I rarely had any contact with the supervisor of the strike force. I knew there was nothing I could do now but wait for the results.

It took about a month for the results of the bid to be official. I was at home when I got a call from a friend from the police department. He told me that the paperwork for the strike force bid was posted, and I was not picked to go. He first told me who the seniority pick was, and that didn't surprise me. I knew he had the most time on the job and he was a good police officer. He then told me who the pick was, and it shocked me. It was Mike, my zone car partner, who worked with Joe and me. I thanked my friend for letting me know and hung up the phone in shock.

I started doing a lot of stinking thinking. I was angry, and I wasn't sure who I should direct my anger at. I remembered what my lieutenant had told me. He said I was going to the strike force. I wondered, what changed? Did the strike force sergeant not pick me because he didn't like me? I thought I would get some answers when I went to work later that day.

On the drive in to work, I prayed, asking God to help me deal with the emotions I was feeling. I knew I could say something that I would regret later. I knew I would see my lieutenant and the strike force sergeant and possibly Mike. I was trying to stay calm.

Even though I was angry, I did know one thing. If God wanted me in the strike force, nothing could have stopped that. I didn't want to pay attention to that thought too long, even though I knew it was the truth. I wondered why God did not want me transferred to the strike force. I wondered, would I have gotten hurt or in trouble, or maybe I would not have enjoyed the job any longer? What I didn't know at this time, God would eventually show me.

I arrived at work and went to my desk and started working. It was hard for me to concentrate. I saw my lieutenant, and he did not say anything about not getting transferred. I thought that was a little weird, because he initially told me I was getting transferred. I figured he would say something. Maybe he was waiting for me to ask him, but I never did. To this day, he has not told me why.

I was working at my desk, trying to avoid any conversation, until I needed to take a bathroom break. I went across the hall into the bathroom, and who did I see? It was the strike force sergeant. We were alone, and I wanted to ask him why he didn't pick me for the job. I could see he was nervous when he saw me.

We both said hello, and I immediately asked him why he didn't pick me for the job. I was hoping he would tell me the truth. Maybe he would tell me I wasn't good enough or qualified. Maybe he would tell me that he didn't like me. He ignored my question and told me that I still had a good job working in the detective bureau. I could see he was stalling, and he didn't want to look directly at me.

The next thing I saw cracked me up. He was using a hand dryer to blow-dry his hands after washing them. The only thing is the hand dryer had been broken for years. He pushed the button, and nothing happened, and he held his hands under the dryer, rubbing them with no air coming out. I looked at him and told him that the hand dryer was broken and asked him why he was trying to dry his hands with no air coming out? I laughed, and he just walked out of the bathroom.

He never did tell me why he didn't pick me. I would have respected him if he had told me he didn't want me to come to the strike force because he personally did not like me. I could understand that. Why work with someone you don't like if you don't have to? To be honest, I really didn't like him or respect him as a police officer, and he probably felt the same about me. I just wanted to work with Joe.

I saw my lieutenant, and he didn't tell me anything, and then I saw the sergeant of the strike force, and he didn't tell me anything, and now the only person left that might know anything was Mike, my old partner. I didn't know how I was going to react when I saw him. Would I congratulate him or ignore the subject with him entirely? I knew it would be awkward and didn't know what I was going to say.

It didn't take long for me to see Mike. When I returned from using the bathroom, Mike was in the detective bureau using the copy machine. Mike was my old partner, and we were friends, but it was hard for me not to be angry and jealous. I felt a little betrayed by him. He did nothing wrong and he had every right to the strike force job.

When Mike saw me, he acted like nothing happened. We talked for a minute, and I congratulated him on getting the job. I really didn't mean it, and maybe my face showed that I didn't mean it. I then told Mike that I got screwed over and I think that the boss of the strike force didn't want me in the unit because he didn't like me. Mike didn't say much after that and left the office. I felt a little better after talking to Mike and after I saw the strike force sergeant. I said what I had to say and now I was done with it. I was making up excuses to make myself feel better, but I really didn't feel any better.

It took me a couple of weeks to begin to feel better. I didn't want to admit it at the time, but the strike force sergeant was right. I still had a good job working in the detective bureau. My thought process changed. I went from anger and jealousy to a calm and peace. The reason I went to a calm and peace was because I wondered what God had in store for me. I believed God would show me the reason why I didn't go to the strike force. I wondered if the strike force job would have affected my marriage negatively or I would have gotten injured. I could have only guessed. Maybe God would show me.

Several months had gone by, and I completely forgot about being passed over for the strike force job. I settled back into my routine. The City of Cleveland had just elected a new mayor, and one of the first things the mayor did was have a financial audit of the city. The audit revealed a $61 million deficit. The new mayor wanted to lay off 700 city workers, including over 200 police officers. The police union argued that the layoffs posed a threat to public safety.

The police department layoffs caused a reduction in some specialized units and some units were eliminated. I wasn't sure how the layoffs would affect me. I had enough seniority, so I knew I wouldn't get laid off. I soon learned that the detective bureau would stay staffed at 100 percent and I was not going to be affected by the layoffs. The next thing I learned was the strike force was going to be shut down completely and the detectives were going to be reassigned back to working in a zone car or possibly moved to the vice unit.

I soon found out that Joe had an opportunity to work in the vice unit during the layoffs, but he decided against that. Joe didn't believe it was right to get transferred without having a bid out for the job. Joe refused the vice job and went back to working a zone car. I respected Joe for making that tough decision; I knew most officers would have chosen the vice job. I must honestly say I'm not sure what I would have done in that situation. That was one of the reasons I wanted to work with Joe. He was thinking of others when most would be trying to take care of themselves.

You are probably wondering why I wanted to write this story about police layoffs and wanting to work in the strike force. When I didn't get the strike force job, I first was angry, and then when I calmed down, I wondered why God didn't let me get the job. I didn't know if God would ever show me the reason. I now believe 100 percent that God knew the layoffs were coming and that the strike force was going to be disbanded. I believe God was protecting me, and at the same time I was being taught a lesson.

What was the lesson I learned? Sometimes, when God says no, it's for our own good. As a parent, have you ever told your kids no? I have, hundreds of times. Why did I say no to my kids? I told them no because at the time I thought what they requested was not good for them or it was inappropriate for their age.

The many times I told my kids no, I was not 100 percent sure if I was correct. My wife and I did the best we could at that time. When God tells you no, you better believe it's the right thing to do. In Jeremiah 29:11, it says, "For I know the plans I have for you," declares the Lord, "plans to prosper you and not to harm you, plans to give you hope and a future."

When I think about Jeremiah 29:11, I realized that God was watching over me and wanted what was best for me. God had my attention. I was once again overwhelmed. Here was the creator of the universe, God Almighty. Why was he taking care of me? Why was he loving me? Why was he letting me witness miracles? I don't want to answer for God, but it says in 1 John 3:1, "See what kind of love the Father has given us, that we should be called children of God; and so, we are. The reason why the world does not know us is that it did not know him."

I believe God is taking care of me because I am his child. I am not perfect, and I still sin, and when I ask for forgiveness, God forgives me. God listens to me no matter where I am or what time of day it is. He guides me and watches over me and protects me and always gives me the correct way to go. There is no one like God. He is my Father, and I am his son. My advice to you is to look for God in every situation, and you will see miracles. You will see how God watches over you. God wants us to pay attention and look for him. What a Father he is.

Chapter 10

Bongo Music

In chapter 9, I wrote about how God was watching out for me. The story I'm writing about now is about how God was watching out for my partner Joe and myself. Joe and I had been working together for about three years. During the three years, we had handled thousands of radio assignments. When you are a police officer, you must be careful not to let routine get in the way of how you handle your assignments. You can get the same alarm drop at a business several times a week because of the wind or a mouse might set the alarm off. This could happen for years, but it is important not to get complacent. Complacency could cost you your life or your partner's life. You cannot take any police assignment for granted.

Joe and I would talk about our tactics and how we could have handled radio assignment safer and tactically to our advantage. We learned from our mistakes. We tried not to do the same thing wrong twice. Joe and I knew each other well. I knew how Joe was going to react, and he knew what I would do. We watched out for each other.

I learned a couple lessons about being complacent early on in my career. I was lucky that nothing serious happened. The first time I learned a big lesson was when I responded to an alarm at a trucking company that I had previously checked with my partner earlier at the beginning of our shift. The second time the alarm went off a few hours later, we were checking the inside of the building. We were going room to room checking every door and any place someone might hide. This time, while checking the building, my partner and I were having a conversation about our families. We were still searching, but our attention was on our conversation.

We checked several rooms and were now in the last room still in conversation. In this room, there was one last closet to check, and I still was talking to my partner about family. When I opened the door to the closet, I was surprised by a man looking at me. Do you remember in the movie *Home Alone* when Kevin McCallister would put his hands on his face and scream? Well, that was what I did. I screamed, and then the man in the closet screamed. If you could've seen us both screaming, you would have had a good laugh.

The second time I learned about being complacent was when I responded to an alarm at a large department store in downtown Cleveland. It was late at night. This store had three floors of merchandise. When my partner and I responded for the alarm, two other zone cars said they would come to assist us. We now had six officers searching the store floor by floor. We checked the store the best we could. It took us about forty-five minutes, and upon completion, we told police radio that the store checked okay inside and outside and it might have been a false alarm. My partner and I left the area and continued back on patrol.

An hour went by, and the department store alarm went off again. This time, police radio said they had motion detected on the first floor of the store. We responded back to the store, and again two other zone cars said they would come to assist us. This time, a police dog handler responded with his dog. I was glad to have a dog help with this search this time. The dog could search a lot better than we could.

We searched the store for a half hour, and again we didn't find anyone or anything that might have set the alarm off. We told police radio that the store again checked okay inside and outside. On the outside of the building, we observed that there were no signs of a forced entry into the store. I felt confident that there wasn't anyone inside the store, especially since the dog was searching with us. We left the store and went back on patrol.

An hour went by, and once again we heard from police radio that the alarm had gone off again. We responded back to the department store and started to check the building once again. This time, only one zone car responded with us to check the building. We went inside the store, and after five minutes of searching, the zone car that assisted us yelled to us that they had caught someone hiding. I couldn't believe it. My partner and I went over to them and saw they had caught a male who was around forty years old.

I asked the arrested male, how did he get inside the store? He told us he was hiding inside a bathroom and waited for the store to close. Once the store closed, he waited for a half hour, and once he had taken what he wanted, he tried to leave the store, but he couldn't get out. He told us that he heard us looking for him two separate times. He said the second time that the police were looking for him, he was hiding under a rack of clothes. He said when he was hiding, a police dog came up to him and licked his face, and then the dog turned around and left. When he told me that, we all started to laugh.

It sure was funny, but this incident taught me another valuable lesson. We had been inside the store three times, and the arrested male was watching us. How dangerous! I also put my trust in a dog. I realized that I took it for granted once the dog had searched the building. I told myself that I would not take any situation for granted.

A couple of months had passed by since we responded to the alarm, and I was working with Joe on second shift. We responded to a police radio assignment. We were told to go to a home and meet a man who was having trouble with his neighbor. He was complaining of loud music that was disturbing him. There was nothing unusual about this type of complaint. It was common for neighbors to argue with each other about music.

It was still light outside when we arrived at the house. We noticed that the house looked like it could be a double or possibly a single house made into a double. We went to the front door, and prior to knocking we waited and listened for any type of loud music. We did not hear any music coming from the house. That wasn't unusual, because if the people playing the loud music saw the police coming, they usually turned it down right away.

We waited for a few minutes at the door, and then we knocked, and an elderly man answered the door. We asked the male if he called the police, and he said he did. I asked him, what was going on? What was the problem? He said that his neighbor was bothering him. He asked us to come upstairs to talk about it. We said, okay, we would. He held the door for us and told us to go up first. That meant that he would be behind us as we walked up the stairs.

When he told us to go upstairs first, I immediately got a bad feeling. He didn't look like a threat at all. He looked more like a grandfather. I told Joe to let him lead the way and we will follow. The man walked up first with Joe, with me behind him. Joe knew what I meant when I told the man to go first. Something was different, and we both knew it. Joe knew I did not trust this man, and neither did Joe. That meant we were going to be on high alert during this interview. No letting our tactical guard down.

Once we were upstairs and inside his house, the man hushed us and said, "Listen, listen, that damn bongo music." Joe and I looked at each other. We didn't hear any music. This man then told us that he rented his downstairs house to a single young female. He then explained that this female had a boyfriend come to the house late at night and played "that damn bongo music." When he spoke about the female, it appeared to Joe and me that he might have feelings for her. We spoke with him for ten minutes and told him we didn't hear any music at this time. We advised him to call us back if the music got loud and bothered him again. I also told him that I would knock on the door and speak to his tenant. As we were leaving, he once again said, "Listen, listen, that damn bongo music."

When we walked down the steps, we made sure to watch our backs. We didn't trust this man even more now after speaking with him. We thought that he was nuts because of the music or his obsession with the female. We weren't sure, but we were not taking any chances.

We knocked on the downstairs door and waited for a response from the female. We thought she might be able to give us a clearer understanding on what was going on. We wanted to ask her about her music and if she played it loud at night. We wanted to know if she had any complaints from her neighbor. Joe and I had worked this zone for three years, and this was the first time we had a complaint at this house. We waited for the female to come to the door for five minutes, but no one responded.

Joe and I walked back to our zone car and left the area and went back patrolling our zone. Inside the car, we talked about this man and wondered if we would get called back to his house again. We also spoke about how he wanted us to walk upstairs with him behind us. We talked about our tactics, and we both agreed that we didn't trust him. That wasn't anything new. There were a lot of people that we had encountered during our workday that we didn't trust. We put it in our memory banks for the future if we ever had to respond to the same house again.

Joe and I went back to the police station, completed our paperwork, and then went home. We were scheduled to work together again the next day on second shift.

For much of my career, I didn't want to bring my job home with me. My wife would ask me if anything interesting happened at work. I would tell her nothing new happened. Over the course of my career, I have told my wife maybe ten police stories. I must laugh now because she must have thought I had a boring job because nothing ever happened. I tell her some stories now that I'm retired. She told me that she had no idea what I did at work. She now gets a little freaked out, and that's why I didn't tell her when it happened. I had no reason to tell her about the damn bongo music man, because nothing happened.

Joe and I arrived for work the next day and went to roll call. While at roll call, we learned that a zone car from day shift responded to a neighbor trouble call. When the police officers arrived and started to walk up to the house, a male started shooting at the officers from inside the house. The officers returned fire and took cover. The officers were not struck by any rounds. The sergeant gave us the address and told us to stay away because SWAT was at the house and it was an active scene.

Joe immediately recognized the address and told the sergeant that we were at that house the day before. We told him about the bongo music and the lady downstairs. Roll call was completed, and Joe and I hurried to go to the area. We knew that the street would be blocked off at each corner with zone cars. We stopped to talk with one of the officers who was blocking the street. He told us that SWAT was negotiating with this male and thought that he was shooting at SWAT officers.

Joe and I had to leave the area to answer police radio calls. We monitored the radio for updates on SWAT. An hour went by, and we heard on the radio that SWAT had to use lethal force on this male and he was now deceased. Joe and I later found it that it was the same male that we had spoken to about loud music the day before.

Joe and I worked the rest of our shift talking about what had just happened. We both realized that it could have been us that this male wanted to kill. We reviewed our tactics from the day prior. What if we had let him walk behind us up the stairs? What if we had let our guard down while we interviewed this male? There was a lot of second-guessing, and we didn't know if this male had plans to ambush us and kill us.

This incident happened over twenty years ago. I can still remember what he looked like and what his home looked like from the inside. I remember the narrow steps going up to his house. I can remember how his voice sounded. The thing I remember the most is how I felt and sensed danger coming from this man. He did not look intimidating at all. He was ordinary-looking and nothing about him appeared threatening. Over the course of my career, I had met thousands of men who were just like him.

It's unusual, when you meet someone for the first time, and less then twenty-four hours later, they are dead, it makes you think. I wondered why I was involved. Why was I supposed to meet this man? I knew it wasn't a coincidence. This is where I believe paying attention is important. God wanted me to meet this man, but why?

I had a lot of time to think about why Joe and I were involved with this man. I waited until all the information came out about this incident. There was nothing unusual. No known mental illness or history of violence. There was nothing known about his past that might have triggered him. I don't know what this man's relationship was with God. Did he even believe in God? That was between him and God.

In Psalm 121:7–8, it says, "The Lord will keep you from all harm; he will watch over your life. The Lord will watch over your coming and going both now and forevermore." I believe God wanted me to realize that he was watching over me. I can look back at this incident and I believe that 100 percent. I believe that this man was going to attempt to ambush Joe and me, but God intervened. In Isaiah 52:12, it says, "But you will not leave in haste or go in flight; for the Lord will go before you, the God of Israel will be your rear guard."

The God of Israel was our rear guard that day. God protecting us should never be taken for granted. I refuse to call it luck. I can look back on my police career, and I can see where God was involved. I believe God was involved in every area. There were times that I disobeyed God and did things on my own, not trusting in what God wanted me to do.

I didn't always pay attention to what God was doing in my life. I can look back on my life now and I can see how God took care of me. There were a lot of dangerous situations working as a police officer. High-speed pursuits with desperate people and hundreds of gun runs. Responding to homicides and suicides. It became routine. No matter what police situation I responded to, I didn't always remember that God was with me. The times I cussed or the times I responded with anger while doing my job. When people were looking to me to act professional, and I acted like a fool. Through it all, God never left me. That's his promise. God says in the Bible that he will never leave us nor forsake us. That bongo music day, God kept his promise. Thank you, Lord. God always pays attention!

Chapter 11

What I Learned about Prayer and Paying Attention

Have you ever wondered if God has heard your prayers? There are many verses in the Bible that speak about prayer. One of my favorite stories in the Bible is in the Book of Daniel in chapter 10. The text says that Daniel received a message from God during the reign of King Cyrus. It spoke about a great war. When Daniel received this message, he was fasting. Daniel fasting is something we need to pay attention to. Fasting is one way to get closer to God and is very important in our prayer life. Fasting will clear your mind and help you to pay attention. I believe this was one of the reasons Daniel was fasting at this time.

In Daniel 10:1–20, it says that in the third year of Cyrus king of Persia, a revelation was given to Daniel.

> The message was true, and it concerned a great war. The understanding of the message came to him in a vision. At that time, I, Daniel, mourned for three weeks. I ate no choice food; no meet or wine touched my lips; and I used no lotions at all until the three weeks were over.
>
> On the twenty-fourth day of the first month, as I was standing on the bank of the great river, the Tigris, I looked up and there before me was a man dressed in linen, with a belt of fine gold from Uphaz around his waist. His body was like topaz, his face like lightning, his eyes like flaming torches, his arms and legs like the gleam of burnished bronze, and his voice like the sound of a multitude.
>
> I, Daniel, was the only one who saw the vision; those who were with me did not see it, but such terror overwhelmed them that they fled and hid themselves. I was left alone, gazing at this great vision; I had no strength left, my face turned

pale and I was helpless. Then I heard him speaking, and as I listened to him, I fell into a deep sleep, my face to the ground.

A hand touched me and set me trembling on my hands and knees. He said, "Daniel, you who are highly esteemed, consider carefully the words I am about to speak to you, and stand up, for I have now been sent to you." And when he said this to me, I stood up trembling.

Then he continued, "Do not be afraid, Daniel. Since the first day that you set your mind gaining understanding and to humble yourself before your God, your words were heard, and I have come in response to them. But the prince of the Persian kingdom resisted me twenty-one days. Then Michael, one of the chief princes, came to help me, because I was detained there with the king of Persia. Now I have come to explain to you what will happen to your people in the future, for the vision concerns a time yet to come."

While he was saying this to me, I bowed with my face toward the ground and was speechless. Then one who looked like a man touched my lips, and I opened my mouth and began to speak. I said to the one standing before me, "I am overcome with anguish because of the vision, my lord, and I feel very weak. How can I, your servant, talk with you, my lord? My strength is gone, and I can hardly breathe."

Again, the one who looked a man touched me and gave me strength. "Do not be afraid, you who are highly esteemed," he said. "Peace! Be strong now; be strong."

When he spoke to me, I was strengthened and said, "Speak, my lord, since you have given me strength."

So, he said, "Do you know why I have come to you? Soon I will return to fight against the prince of Persia, and when I go the prince of Greece will come; but first I will tell you what is written in the Book of Truth."

This part of the Bible shows how Daniel was paying attention. There are two important points to remember, and we need to pay attention to what Daniel was doing. Daniel was fasting and praying for twenty-one days. Look at what it says in Daniel 10:12: "Do not be afraid, Daniel.

Since the first day that you set your mind to gain understanding and to humble yourself before God, your words were heard, and I have come in response to them."

Those words spoken directly from heaven to Daniel are comforting to me, and they should be a comfort to you. We need to realize that God hears our prayers. When we pray and ask God to consider our prayer request, do we take it for granted? Do we give the glory to God? Do you believe that God hears your words like he heard Daniel's?

In Daniel's vision, he was told that he was highly esteemed. How do you become highly esteemed? The definition of *esteemed* is one who is admired and held in great respect. Daniel was fasting and praying for twenty-one days. This might be one way to be identified as highly esteemed by God. It also said that Daniel had set his mind to gain understanding and humbled himself. It looks like all these characteristics are important.

I must be honest with myself. I have never felt like I was highly esteemed in God's eyes. I don't know if Daniel felt like he was highly esteemed before he was told he was. The important thing to remember is what Daniel was doing prior to this vision. Daniel had set his mind to gain understanding and he humbled himself. This is a great example for us. We need to follow Daniel's example.

Would you like God to look at you and give you a compliment or answer your prayers? Try fasting and praying. There are several stories in the Bible where God had answered prayer during a fast. Jesus fasted for forty days and nights. If Jesus fasted, we should at least attempt a fast and follow Jesus's example.

In the history of mankind, there has been no one humbler than Jesus Christ. Daniel did not have Jesus Christ's example on how to be humble, yet God said he was humble. The good thing is we have Jesus as an example for us on how to be humble. If we follow Jesus's example, we can't go wrong.

When I read the Bible, I gain understanding. When I listen to the Holy Spirit, I gain understanding. When I attend church and listen to a sermon, I gain understanding. When I watch other Christians and how they respond in stressful situations, I gain understanding. Most importantly, when I follow Jesus, I gain understanding. I'm not sure how Daniel gained understanding, but I would bet if he lived during or after Jesus that he too would have looked to Jesus for understanding.

The important thing to remember is God first. In the Bible in Matthew 6:33, it says, "But seek ye first the kingdom of God, and his righteousness; and all these things shall be added unto you." Now that is something to pay attention to!

Chapter 12

God Was Paying Attention to Me

I am now sixty-four years old. I look back at my life, and I can see where God was watching over me. When I was younger, in my teens, I remember several critical times where I cried out to God and asked for help because my life was falling apart. The trouble I got into was because of my sins. I would tell God that I was sorry, and I wouldn't do it again. Sometimes I got away with my sin, and sometimes I didn't.

What I know now is that you never get away with sin. Back then, I believed God would come into my life and solve my problems, and then leave. I did not have a real relationship with God. If you're a parent, you probably understand about having a relationship with your children. How would you like it if the only time your children spoke to you was when they got into trouble? That wouldn't be much of a relationship. As parents, we would be hurt, but we would still help our kids because we love them. After we helped our children, we would probably give them advice on how to stay out of trouble for the next time. If the kids continued to do the same thing, how would that make you feel? I know I would feel used.

I was using God only when I needed him. This continued all the way into my twenties. I continued to sin and get into trouble. During this time of trouble, several people would give me advice on how to change my life. Even though I had good friends and family for support, I felt alone and depressed. I wasn't paying attention to anything, especially God.

I remember during this time, I had met several strangers who witnessed to me and told me about Jesus and how to have a relationship with him. I listened and resisted. I realize now that God had sent these people to me. God even used my best friend Ken to talk to me about church and what I believed about God. Ken told me that his niece Sandy was attending church and she had changed tremendously. He said Sandy's mother was worried about her because Sandy would fall asleep on her knees during prayer. Ken then asked me if I wanted to visit the church that Sandy attended on a Thursday night. I accepted the invitation. I wanted to know what changed Sandy.

Thursday could not come soon enough. Ken picked me up for church, and when we arrived, I was shocked to see hundreds of cars in the parking lot. For a Thursday night, I was amazed. We went inside and found Sandy. We sat together. The church was crowded, but everyone seemed friendly.

The church service started with some music. I was amazed to see how excited the people were during the music. I knew immediately that this service was going to be different. Some people were lifting their hands up praising God. I had never seen this type of service before. I wasn't sure what to do, so I didn't do anything. I just watched.

The music ended, and the pastor of the church came up to the podium. The pastor's first name was Bob. He wore a suit and tie and carried a Bible in his hand. Pastor Bob started to preach to the crowd. I started to feel uncomfortable. I felt like he was talking directly to me. I couldn't believe it. I wondered who told the pastor I was coming to church and who told him everything that I was feeling and what I was going through. I later learned that no one told the pastor about me.

I now know who told Bob I was at the service and what needed to be said. It was the Holy Spirit. In Bob's sermon, he spoke a lot about Jesus. He said never did a man speak like Jesus. He spoke about salvation and needing a savior. Bob spoke about how Jesus died for our sins, and there was only one way to God and that was through his Son Jesus. He spoke about Jesus's miracles and how he defeated death and rose from the dead after being crucified on a cross. A lot of what Bob was saying I knew but I didn't pay attention prior. Tonight was different, and I knew it. I was paying attention.

At the end of the service, Bob asked everyone to bow our heads and close our eyes. Bob then said, "If you want to accept Jesus into your life, please raise your hand." I wanted to raise my hand, but I was still resisting. Bob then recited a salvation prayer and asked the people who raised their hand to come forward so he could give them a New Testament Bible. I watched as several people walked to the front of the church. I wasn't one of them. I was afraid of what people would think.

After the service, I rode home with Ken, and we spoke about what we had just experienced. We both enjoyed the service, and I told him I wanted to go back next week. We also spoke about Sandy and her commitment to prayer and church.

Ken drove me to my house, and before I left, he invited me to a picnic with his family on the upcoming Saturday. He told me Sandy and her family were going to be there. I accepted his invitation and I thought that it would be a good time to talk with Sandy about God and prayer. I wanted to see if Sandy was for real. I was now paying attention to Sandy. Non-Christians do that sometimes. We pay attention to Christians because we want to see if they still sin. Are they hypocrites? I would find out more on Saturday.

I arrived at the picnic, and I was looking forward to talking with Sandy. I saw her sitting at a picnic table alone. I hardly knew Sandy. I had seen her a few times at Ken's house and we hardly ever spoke to each other. I walked over to her, and when I got close, I noticed that she had brought her Bible with her. I had no idea how I was going to start a conversation with her about God.

Sandy asked me if I enjoyed church Thursday night. I told her I did enjoy it, but it was not what I was used to. I felt a little funny and awkward because my intent was to find out if she was for real. While we were talking, I asked Sandy if I could look at her Bible. She said yes. That was the first time I ever picked up a Bible and opened it. We continued talking while I was turning pages. What I saw in her Bible completely blew me away.

Sandy had notebook paper in her Bible, and on the paper, she had written down names of people whom she was praying for and the reasons for prayer. Sandy didn't know that I was looking at her prayer list. About halfway down the list, I saw my name and how she was praying for me. I quickly shut the Bible and gave it back to her. I talked with Sandy for another ten minutes, then left.

I couldn't stop thinking about someone I hardly knew praying for me. I wondered how she knew about what to pray for. I figured Ken must have told her that I was going through a rough time in my life. I now understood why Sandy would fall asleep on her knees praying. Sandy was paying attention. She was paying attention to everyone. Paying attention to help through prayer.

On Sunday morning, I was still thinking about attending church on Thursday and how the pastor spoke about salvation. Sandy praying for me was also in my head. I started thinking about my life and how it was such a mess. I wanted to change who I was and what I had become. I knew that I needed God in my life, and I needed to ask God for forgiveness.

I got down on my knees, and I remember crying and asking God to forgive me and to come into my life. This was my all-in moment. I knew it was trusting God 100 percent, no turning back. I knew I was going to be different.

When I got up from my knees, I knew that God had forgiven me, and I was a changed man. This is how I felt. God forgave me for everything, and I was given a fresh new start. In 2 Corinthians 5:17, it says, "Therefore if anyone is in Christ, he is a new creation. The old has passed away; behold the new has come." I was a new creation, and I was excited about my new life to come. There is nothing better in this world than to know you are forgiven, with no strings attached. Jesus dying on the cross gave me a second chance. This new start to my life was going to be different.

I immediately knew that I no longer wanted to sin, and I wanted a relationship with God.

I wanted to learn more about Jesus immediately. I knew the best place to learn about Jesus was in the Bible. I didn't own a Bible, so I wanted to buy one as soon as possible. I realized that on the corner of the street where I lived was a Christian bookstore. It was a small building, and the owner had recently opened the store. I had passed by that store hundreds of times and rarely saw any customers inside. I had never been inside the store. I now believe that God put that store there for me.

I went inside the store and looked around. I told the owner that I was a new Christian and I wanted to get a Bible. He directed me to some Bibles and recommended a book about holiness. I bought a Bible and the book the owner recommended and went back home.

I was excited to start reading the Bible. I started in the New Testament. I couldn't put the Bible down. The words came to life, and the more I read the more I felt like God's words were giving me strength. I read for a couple of hours, and I realized that I wanted to be a different man. I knew God had changed me and forgiven me. I had a new life ahead. I wondered what God had planned for me.

I was so excited about God and I wanted to tell everyone I knew about salvation and how God had forgiven me, a sinner. I told all my friends and family about how I accepted Christ as my Savior. I initially thought that they would want the same for their lives, but that was not the case. Most of the people I spoke to about Jesus thought I was nuts or one of those Jesus freaks. I wasn't nuts, but I was a Jesus freak. I loved Jesus and I was thankful that he came to die for me and anyone else who put their trust in him. My life was changed. Jesus said, "I have come that they might have life, and that they may have it more abundantly."

My life was changing, and one thing I noticed was that my family and friends were starting to pay attention to me. I read the book about holiness that I purchased with the Bible. The author spoke about getting rid of anything in your life that the devil could get glory out of. When I finished reading the book, I looked around my house and saw several things I needed to get rid of. When I was done cleaning up my house, I was amazed at how many things I had gotten rid of. I had taken sin for granted and now I wanted to start paying attention to my new life. I felt that God was paying attention to me.

When I attended school, I was not a good student. It was hard for me to read and comprehend. I would have to reread a paragraph several times and maybe I would eventually understand what I read. I knew that I wanted to know everything about God and how to apply what was written in the Bible to my life. I wanted God to direct me on how to live my life. I was shocked when I started to read the Bible and I understood what I was reading. I believe God took that confusion away from my reading.

When I read the Bible, I understood why Jesus came to earth. The most important point is he came as a Savior for those who put their trust in him. Jesus also showed us how to live. There is no one like Jesus. Think about that. I will say it again. There is no one like Jesus. If you want to pay attention to anything in life, pay attention to what Jesus said and did. Jesus promises us that he will never leave us or forsake us. It doesn't matter what time of day it is or where you are. Jesus is available to talk with us and listen twenty-four hours a day, seven days a week, and 365 days a year. Tell me he is not paying attention to us. He is, and he is faithful.

I have been saved since 1982, and I can honestly say that Jesus was with me since the first day I got saved. He has taken the time to comfort me in times of trouble and calm the storm when I felt like I was alone. You can take this to the bank. Jesus is not caught off guard or surprised about anything that is going on in your life. Jesus is not in heaven running around not knowing what to do. Jesus knows everything. Jesus is paying attention to us. Aren't you glad he is? Right now, we should take the time to thank him.

Chapter 13

Strategy for Paying Attention

My first suggestion for paying attention would be to start a relationship with Jesus. If Jesus was here on earth right now and he was preaching at a church, would you want to go? If you answered yes to that question, then you should ask yourself why. I know why I would want to go. Jesus's words changes lives. Jesus's words are healing. Jesus's words save lives. I believe if you went to see Jesus, you would be paying attention.

I believe that there would be millions of people waiting in line to hear Jesus speak. It would be world headline news. If you went to listen to Jesus, and his words changed you, and you wanted to start a relationship with him, what would you do? I know what I would want to do. When Jesus finished speaking and left, I would attempt to follow him. I would want to know where he was staying or where he was speaking next. If I ever had a chance to speak with him face-to-face, I would ask him if I could go with him. I would want to learn everything about him. If Jesus said yes, then I would pay attention to everything Jesus did and everything Jesus said.

How do you think Jesus would impact your life? We must remember that Jesus is God and he is holy. Jesus never sinned. Jesus never lied. Every word Jesus spoke was the truth. Can you tell me anyone else since the beginning of time who always spoke the truth and never lied? The answer is no. We should think about that. If you asked Jesus any question, you would always get the truth. That is something to pay attention to; Jesus always tells the truth.

Now, we need to be honest with ourselves. Do you have a relationship with Jesus? Do you want to be a follower of Jesus? Do you believe Jesus's words are all the truth? If you answered yes, then it's time to go all in and follow Jesus like he was here, right now, on earth. Now is the time to pay attention.

Jesus is our Savior. Ask for forgiveness for our sins and repent. Ask Jesus to come into our lives so we can have a relationship. I wouldn't swap my salvation for a million dollars, because it's priceless.

My second suggestion for paying attention is to start reading the Bible. The Bible is God speaking to us. There are so many examples about how to live your life. The first example of man's sin and the consequences were Adam and Eve. Once Adam and Eve sinned, their life changed. Almost immediately, God confronted Adam and Eve about their sin. Guess what happened next because of sin. God evicted them from the Garden of Eden, and their lives were never the same.

Being a police officer, I was amazed to learn when and where the very first homicide took place and what the motive was. Adam and Eve had two sons named Cain and Abel. When the brothers were older, Cain killed his brother because he was jealous. Almost immediately, God confronted Cain about his sin. God asked Cain, where is his brother Abel? Cain said, "Am I my brother's keeper?" This was the very first homicide interview. God knew what happened to Abel. Imagine being interviewed by God.

There is nothing that happens in this world and our life that God doesn't know about. The Old Testament has awesome stories about God and the people who trusted in him. There are so many miracles and acts of faith for us to draw strength from. There are also many examples of sin and its consequences where we can learn from other people's mistakes.

Some of my favorite stories in the Old Testament are about insurmountable odds. People who had put their trust and faith in God. Do you remember David killing Goliath? That fight didn't last too long. When David and Goliath squared off to fight, Goliath realized his opponent was a young boy and he felt insulted. Goliath said to David, "Am I a dog that you come at me with sticks?" Goliath then cursed at him by his gods. Goliath then said, "Come here, and I'll give your flesh to the birds and the wild animals!" Guess how David responded?

David said, "You come against me with sword and spear and javelin, but I come against you in the name of the Lord Almighty, the God of the armies of Israel, whom you have defied. This day the Lord will deliver you into my hands, and I'll strike you down and cut off your head. This very day I will give the carcasses of the Philistine army to the birds and the wild animals, and the whole world will know that there is a God of Israel. All those gathered here will know that it is not by sword or spear that the Lord saves; for the battle is the Lord's, and he will give all of you into our hands."

What prefight hype. If this happened today, it would be on pay-per-view. I would bet that 100 percent of the money wagered would be on Goliath. You would probably have to bet a million dollars to get one hundred dollars. One of the best parts of this story is there were a lot of witnesses to what was said.

We all know what happened next. David used his slingshot and hit Goliath directly in the forehead and Goliath fell face-down dead before he hit the ground. David then took Goliath's sword and cut off the giant's head.

There is another story I love in the Old Testament. This story is about Moses and Pharaoh. The Israelites were slaves of Pharaoh. God told Moses to go and talk with Pharaoh and tell him to free the Israelites. Pharaoh was stubborn and initially refused. God sent several plagues on Egypt, and only after the killing of all the firstborns did Pharaoh allow the Israelites to depart from slavery.

In the Bible in Exodus 14, God told Moses what to do. It went like this. The Lord said to Moses, "Tell the Israelites to turn back and encamp near Pi Hahiroth, between Migdol and the sea. They are to encamp by the sea, directly opposite Baal Zephon. Pharaoh will think, 'The Israelites are wandering around the land in confusion, hemmed in by the desert,' and I will harden Pharaoh's heart, and he will pursue them. But I will gain glory for myself through Pharaoh and all his army, and the Egyptians will know that I am the Lord."

When the king of Egypt was told that the people had fled, Pharaoh and his officials changed their minds about them and said, "What have we done? We have let the Israelites go and have lost their services!"

The Egyptians and all Pharaoh's horses and chariots, horsemen and his troops pursued Moses and the Israelites. When Pharaoh approached, the Israelites looked up, and there were the Egyptians, marching after them. They were terrified and cried out to the Lord. Moses told the people not to be afraid. "Stand firm and you will see the deliverance the Lord will bring you today. The Egyptians you see today you will never see again. The Lord will fight for you; you need only to be still."

The Lord told Moses to tell the Israelites to keep moving. He instructed Moses to raise his staff and stretch out his hand over the sea to divide the water so that the Israelites can go through on dry ground. Moses stretched out his hand over the sea, and all night the Lord drove the sea back with a strong east wind and turned it into dry land. The waters were divided, and the Israelites went through the sea on dry ground, with a wall of water on either side.

The Egyptians pursued them, and all Pharaoh's chariots and horsemen followed them into the sea. The Lord then threw the Egyptian army into confusion.

The Lord then told Moses to stretch out his hand over the sea so that the waters may flow back over the Egyptians and their chariots and horsemen. Moses stretched out his hand over the sea, and at daybreak the sea went back to its place. The Egyptians were swept into the sea. The entire army of Pharaoh that followed the Israelites were all dead. Not one survivor.

The Old Testament has a lot of stories about God answering prayer and intervening to help in desperate situations. I believe God still answers prayers today. David and Moses had everything against them. They should not have come out on top, but they did. Read the Old Testament and claim God's power in your life. Pay attention to their faith. Trust God.

My third suggestion is to read the New Testament. Once Jesus was born, people started paying attention to him. Jesus was performing miracles. He had raised the dead and healed the sick. Jesus had calmed a storm and the apostles were amazed and asked, "What kind of man is this? Even the winds and the waves obey him!" We should be asking this same question.

In the Bible in Luke 8:43–48, Jesus healed a woman who was subject to bleeding for twelve years and no one could heal her. In this story, there was a crowd of people around Jesus pressing up against him. This lady with the bleeding touched the edge of Jesus's cloak, and immediately her bleeding stopped. Jesus said, "Who touched me?" Peter told Jesus that the crowd was pressing against him. Jesus said, "Someone touched me; I know the power has gone out of me." The woman saw she could not go unnoticed; she came trembling and fell at his feet. She told Jesus why she had touched him and how she had been instantly healed. Jesus said to her, "Daughter, your faith has healed you. Go in peace."

Did you pay attention to what Jesus told her? It was her faith that healed her. There is another thing to pay attention to during this miracle. Sometimes we feel we are all alone in a crowd and other people might be more important than us. Jesus singled her out. Do you know why? I believe that Jesus pays attention to our faith. At this time, we need to ask ourselves, *How much faith do I have?*

Another example of faith that Jesus spoke about is in Luke 7:1–10. It says that after Jesus had finished saying all this to the people who were listening, he entered Capernaum. There a centurion's servant, whom his master valued highly, was sick and about to die. The centurion heard of Jesus and sent some elders of the Jews to him, asking him to come and heal his servant. When they came to Jesus, they pleaded earnestly with him, "This man deserves to have you do this, because he loves out nation and has built our synagogue." So, Jesus went with them.

He was not far from the house when the centurion sent friends to say to him: "Lord, don't trouble yourself, for I do not deserve to have you come under my roof. That is why I did not even consider myself worthy to come to you. But say the word, and my servant will be healed. For I myself am a man under authority, with soldiers under me. I tell this one, 'Go', and he goes; and that one, 'Come,' and he comes. I say to my servant, 'Do this,' and he does it."

When Jesus heard this, he was amazed at him, and turning to the crowd following him, he said, "I tell you, I have not found such great faith even in Israel." Then the men who had been sent returned and found the servant well.

Did you pay attention to what Jesus said? He said he did not find such great faith even in Israel. From Jesus's statement, it appears that he is paying attention to us. Jesus is looking at us to see how much we trust him. If Jesus was speaking about you, what would he say about your faith? Would Jesus say, "I have not found such great faith even in Ohio," or wherever you live? Would Jesus be amazed at your faith?

Right now, make a commitment to have faith in God 100 percent. Read what Jesus said in the Bible and apply his words to your life.

My fourth suggestion is to have a life plan. You can start right now. I would begin by having a conversation with God. Ask God, "What do you want me to accomplish today?" You should also create a written prayer list. I learned this from Sandy. Write down the names of people that God wants you to pray for along with the reasons. Start paying attention to what is going on around you during your day. If someone tells you that they are having some type of problem in their life, tell them you will pray for them. Sometimes you could stop and pray with them right away.

How many times has a friend told you about a pending divorce or a drug-addicted child or some other problem? Get involved and tell them about Jesus. Tell them the stories that you have read in the Bible. Let them see that you trust Jesus and you have faith. What you will learn when someone tells you about their trouble is that God sent them to you. We must be alert when God sends people to talk with us. We must be ready at any moment. It's not an accident that someone confides in you about their problems.

If you are a Christian who pays attention to what is going on around you every day, you will have so much joy and fun. You will see miracles. You will see lives changed. When God is your leader, anything is possible.

We need to believe everything about God. Our God can do anything. When praying, do not limit what God is capable of. Jesus healed the sick and raised the dead. He turned water into wine. He walked on water and controlled the weather. Jesus not only did miracles but through him lives were changed forever by what he said to the people he met.

Tell people about Jesus's miracles, but, more importantly, tell them what he said. Jesus's words changed lives. We should try to memorize what Jesus said.

When you think about your life plan with God, try one day at a time. Send someone a text and tell them that you will be praying for them all day or all week. Tell them that you are expecting a miracle. Call a friend and ask them this question: "How can I pray for you today?" People will start paying attention when they know that you care about them.

There are times when you will want to be more focused on your relationship with God. Life can speed up and make us crazy. My suggestion: if you are medically able, try a fast. There are a lot of books on fasting. Give your fast a theme. One example might be praying for your children. Another example is asking God for direction in your life. Make sure to pray while fasting. When you want to eat something, pray instead. Fasting will bring you closer to God and help you to pay attention.

Set examples. Pray about everything. When you eat a meal, pray with your family. It doesn't have to be a long prayer. Tell God, "Thank you for the food." When you're in your car, pray for protection while driving. Ask for a safe trip. How many times have you had close calls where someone has just missed hitting you with their car? I have friends who give thanks to God when they get a green light instead of a red light. Do not take anything for granted. Make an effort to keep in contact with God throughout the day. We need to remember what God promised us. He said, "I will never leave you or forsake you."

When you pray, start looking for the results. Do not take it for granted. Sometimes the answer to your prayer can be immediate, and other times it can take years.

Remember, it's God's timing and not our timing. God's timing is perfect. I believe when you start to pay attention, you will witness miracles from God.

Chapter 14

This Is Not about Me

When I told my wife that I wanted to write a book, she encouraged me to write about what I knew best. I knew how to be a policeman. I remembered hundreds of stories during my career. Every type of crime you could imagine, I had witnessed or responded to. I didn't want to write another book about crime. I thought about the stories that I told to friends and family, and sometimes strangers. The police stories that I told the most were the stories that I wrote about in this book. Very rarely did I speak about any of my other police experiences.

My wife, Laura, has heard the stories so many times now and could probably recite them word for word. I loved telling how God solved crime. I enjoyed watching the faces of people when I told them that I prayed and that, almost immediately, God answered my prayer. When I told my friends from church, they were amazed. When I told strangers, they would be amazed, but I don't think they believed God was always involved. I think they believed it was just a coincidence.

My intention, when I told the stories and when I wrote this book, was always to give glory to God. I did not want the people to look at me like I was some type of super policeman. I wanted people to look to God. If the person I told the stories to was not a believer in Christ, I used the stories for an opening to witness. I was hoping that they would see my faith in God as a positive.

There are blessings when I told people about the miracles. Sometimes I would hear stories about their experiences with God. Countless times, I was amazed how God healed someone who had been diagnosed with cancer or some other disease. Parents prayed for their children and their drug addiction, and God healed their kids. People prayed and survived accidents and near-death experiences.

In all the miracles that these people spoke about, they always gave glory to God. They were happy that they were witness to a miracle, but they were always humble. For me, that was something to pay attention to.

Chapter 15

Look for a Miracle

Have you ever watched the news on television where the reporter was at a crime scene? If you have, you might have noticed prayer vigils. Never again take these prayer vigils for granted. You can join in prayer and ask God for answers. Write down your request. Do you remember a crime that was reported on television and has not yet been solved? Start praying.

A friend's daughter, named Leslie, was murdered in Bedford Heights in the 1980s, and to this day, the case has not been solved. You can help right now and make a commitment to prayer. Ask God to let it be known who killed this innocent child. God knows who did this.

JonBenét Ramsey was murdered in 1996, and the crime has never been solved. God knows who killed this little girl. Ask God to reveal who is responsible.

One of the most important things we can do is pray for the police. Pray for the detectives who are responsible for these investigations. Ask God to direct them and help them to look at every possible lead. Ask God that if there are no more investigative leads, to please let a reluctant witness come forward. Ask God to have the persons who committed these crimes not have one day of peace until they are captured.

You might be surprised to know how many police officers look to God in prayer and ask for help solving crime. I know this firsthand. I have met a lot of Christian police officers who trust in God. I have seen several officers who would give victims money or food or clothing. I have seen police officers help the homeless.

Why do you think these police officers helped? I believe that it was answered prayer. God heard the prayers of mothers and fathers praying for their children or loved ones. How many parents have prayed and asked God to send someone to their kids because of addiction or homelessness? When you see strangers helping strangers, you are witnessing a miracle. God is answering prayers.

Don't quit, don't stop praying. Look for the answers. Look for miracles. Why pray? God answers prayers, that's why.

Chapter 16

Prayer Unit

There are many specialized units within the police department. The homicide unit investigates murder. Wouldn't it be nice if every homicide investigated were solved? The sex crime unit investigates all types of rape against adults and children. The auto theft unit investigates stolen vehicles. Unit detectives investigate aggravated robberies and break-ins and many other felony crimes. The narcotic unit investigates all types of drug-related crime. There are many other specialized units within the police department. Thousands of crimes are reported and investigated every year. Sad to say, but not all crime is solved.

I wondered what would happen if a chief of police created a prayer unit. The unit would consist of men and women from the police department who would meet weekly. The officers would review unsolved crimes and then pray for the victims and then ask God for guidance on how to proceed.

If I was the chief of police, I would start with all the cold-case homicides. Remember, God knows everything. Do you remember when I wrote about God solving the first homicide? Cain killed Abel. God wanted that first homicide solved. Why wouldn't he want to help us solve other homicides? I believe he would.

You do not have to be a police officer to start a prayer unit. I would suggest you get involved by creating your own group of prayer warriors. After getting the prayer group together, I would contact the chief of police and set up a meeting. Once you meet with the chief, you could ask how the group could help with prayer. Ask the chief to give the group a couple of cold cases, maybe homicides. I understand that the chief cannot give out certain types of case information. I'm sure that he could give a victim name and location. The media usually already gives out that type of information.

What next? Pray and wait for the results. I believe you will start to see God working through you and through the police. Pay attention and write your prayer request down. The chief will know what the prayer unit is praying about and he will obviously see results.

When you see results, please let me know.

Chapter 17

The End and the Beginning

When I retired from the police department, my friends asked me what I was going to do with all my free time. My wife was still working and had several years before she could retire. My children were older and living on their own. I have always exercised and had recently learned how to play pickleball. I knew I had ambitions to write a book. I figured with exercise and writing, that would help to kill time until my wife retired.

What I didn't realize until I started writing my book was that God prepared me for the end of my police career. It is hard for police officers to let go of the adrenaline rush and excitement that they experience daily. How do you substitute for vehicle pursuits or a foot chase when a suspect has just committed a crime? I wondered if I would be able to make the change from police to civilian.

It's funny to think now about when I was a rookie police officer. I remember my first few days riding with my training officer. I recall a civilian female waving at us while we were driving down the street. I waved back at the lady, thinking she was waving hello. My training officer immediately turned the car around and stopped to talk with this female. This lady had just been victimized. After we finished interviewing this lady, I told my training officer what I was thinking. I told him that I forgot that I was a policeman sitting in a police car. I felt like I was just riding around with a friend. I didn't realize who I was yet. I was a civilian all my life, and now I was in uniform carrying a gun.

Eventually, you must become aware of who you are and what your job responsibilities are. As the years went by, I knew I was a police officer. I learned to look for crime. I didn't make the mistake of thinking that someone waving to me was them saying hello. I knew the difference. During an eight-hour shift, you had to stay alert and be prepared to respond to any situation. During my career, I believe that I have experienced evil in all forms. The evil I saw changed me. I was no longer a civilian riding around in a car enjoying the view.

The bad part of being a police officer is that you are never off duty. I tried not to bring the job home with me, but that didn't always work out. I noticed that my habits changed. I became very cautious everywhere I went with my family. No matter where I went, I carried my gun. When I drove in my vehicle to a location, I would watch people on the street and in their cars. The same habits I had while working, I carried them over when I was off duty. I didn't let my guard down. I felt that if I slacked off tactically, something bad could happen to my family and me.

My wife, the schoolteacher, taught me a lesson about being on duty when I was on my days off. At times when we were together taking a ride in our car, I would notice a vehicle that I thought might be stolen. I would tell my wife that I think the car was stolen. I did this several times a year, until one time my wife kept me in check.

We were driving to a restaurant when she saw a young boy standing at a crosswalk. We were waiting for the light to change when she asked me if I saw the boy. I told her yes. She said to me, "I don't think that kid knows how to read." I didn't understand. She explained to me that I constantly look for criminal activity when I was out with her. She told me that she doesn't bring her work home, so I should try to do the same.

My wife was right. I knew I had to change how I was affecting my family. From my experiences, I had built up so many precautions for my family. I realized that I was no longer that rookie who waved hello to a victim who needed help.

I never 100 percent stopped being a cautious husband or father. I always paid attention but kept a lot of my thoughts to myself. As my career continued, I learned more and more about evil and attempted to understand from interviews why people do the things they do. I got pretty good at reading body language. There was good and bad about body language. The good was helpful when I did criminal interviews. The bad was when I analyzed friends and family conversations. After having a conversation with my friends, I wondered, why were they lying to me? I'm laughing now, but would you want to be my friend?

I want you to know that from the first day that I became a police officer, I was a Christian. I know I evolved and became skeptical and distrusted everyone. God was the only one I trusted. I believe that from the very first day I became a Christian God had a plan for me.

God knew I was going to be a police officer. He also knew what direction my career would follow. He had control over it all. He knew I was going to meet Anna and buy her house. He knew I was going to get involved with a doughnut shop robbery. He knew I was going to investigate the jewelry store, and he put the person responsible handcuffed to my desk. He knew I was going to meet Dave and find his stolen bike, and he knew things in the other stories that I wrote about.

While I was transitioning from being a civilian to a police officer, God was changing me. I went from being an overcautious tactical police officer, father, and husband, to a Christian man who happened to be a police officer. God showed me his way of doing things. Once I realized that God was in control of my life and nothing that I did could change that, my life became much more exciting. I would get excited going to work wondering what God had in store for me. I have heard that if you love your job, you will never work a day in your life. If you add God to that statement, it becomes a million times better.

On my last day of work, I left with no regrets. I knew that this was the end. On the ride home, on that last day, I thought about my career in law enforcement. I realized that God was with me the whole time. When I did wrong and didn't trust God, I felt God always taught me a lesson. The lessons I learned about anger and being able to say, "I'm sorry, I was wrong," are priceless. I knew that I didn't always act properly during my career. When God teaches us a lesson, it's always to make us a better person. I also thought about God answering my prayers and allowing me to witness miracles. I realized that God had watched over and protected me during hundreds of dangerous police assignments. On the way home, I prayed, thanking God, and wondered, what do I do now? Was this the end?

I didn't do anything for the first week of my retirement. I still wanted to exercise by playing pickleball, so I joined a tennis club. The next thing I did was buy a computer. I bought the computer so I could start to write my book. My wife was going to work during the day, so I figured I could write while she was away. I thought that I would be able to finish my book in six months. I'm laughing now because it took me almost four years.

I did learn something new while writing my book on the computer. I realized that when I was in high school in the '70s, I took a typing class for a couple of years. The only reason I took typing in high school was because most of the students were female and I thought it would be an easy class to pass. When I completed the typing courses, I could type around 55 words a minute. I believe now that God knew I was going to use a computer to type a book, and I needed to know the keyboard. That was over forty years ago. God was preparing me for the future, and I had no idea until now.

There was another way God was preparing me for the future. God saw a need for our church to have a security team. I was able to identify several church members who wanted to protect our membership. We now have a team that will be able to respond to an active shooter in our church.

Our church does have a modest benevolent fund. My pastor has asked me to be part of this team. My job is to interview strangers that come to our church for assistance. Believe it or not, there are people who will come to a church and ask for money and their intentions are not truthful. During the interviews, I try to establish if our church can help. I believe God was preparing me for this when I was a detective. I had done thousands of interviews while in the detective bureau and had to figure out if the person being interviewed was being truthful.

When I was a police officer, I knew what my mission was. Now that I'm retired, I have a new mission. I wondered, would I still see miracles? The answer is yes. Our church has a prayer board. On this board it says, "Prayer is the engine of our church." The board has notepaper with prayer requests written on it. The requests ask for healing of the sick or for relationships and jobs. Drug addiction and alcoholism are prayed for. Many different prayer requests. The board also shows prayers that were recently answered. I am seeing miracles.

I realize that my career with the police department has ended. I have one question to ask myself: *Do you know what today is?* For me, it's the beginning. Every new day is the beginning. I get my cases from God, and God doesn't need a badge.

This is my ending prayer, and my beginning prayer.

Dear Lord, thank you for watching and protecting me during my career. Thank you for the lessons you taught me. Thank you for letting me work in a job that I loved. I know it's not the end of my work here on earth. Please continue to use me. I ask today that you send me to one person whom you have identified, that I can tell them about you and what you did for me.

Thank you.

Rick

About the Author

Rick Maruniak has been in law enforcement for thirty years. His career began as a Military Police Officer in the Army, stationed in Germany in 1973. He later worked as a 911 police radio operator in the City of Cleveland. He became a Cleveland Police Officer in 1989 and eventually worked his way to becoming a detective with Cleveland. Rick then took the promotional test and was promoted to sergeant. Once he became a sergeant, he was able to transfer to the SWAT unit. In the last four years of his career, he worked in the Internal Affairs Unit.

Rick and his wife, Laura, have been married thirty-two years and have two children, Joseph and Molly.

Rick has been a Christian since 1982.